The RELATIONSHIP

Knowing Jesus Beyond Religion

A Spiritual Biography by

DAVID ANGERON

Published by:

John Melvin Publishing, LLC

123 N. Parkerson Ave.

Crowley, LA 70526

www.johnmelvinpublishing.com

ISBN: 979-8-9948670-1-3 (Paperback)

ISBN: 979-8-9948670-2-0 (Hardback)

Printed in the United States of America

TABLE OF CONTENTS

ACKNOWLEDGEMENTS

This book would not exist without the grace of God and the people He placed in my life at the right moments.

First and foremost, I thank **Jesus Christ**—not as a concept or a religious figure, but as a living, present Savior who met me in brokenness and patiently taught me what a real relationship looks like. This journey has been one of grace, restoration, and daily surrender, and everything in these pages flows from learning to walk with Him rather than merely know about Him.

I am profoundly grateful for my wife, **Jean Melvin Angeron**. Her faith has been steady when mine wavered, honest when mine was confused, and rooted in relationship when mine was still tangled in religion. She consistently pointed me—not toward rules, performance, or appearances—but toward a genuine, personal walk with Jesus. Her love, patience, wisdom, and spiritual discernment helped guide me back to what matters most, and this book bears her influence in countless ways.

To my **children**, thank you for your grace, your patience, and your love. You have taught me more about humility, forgiveness, and unconditional love than you will ever know. My prayer is that you pursue Jesus not out of obligation or tradition, but out of a real, living relationship that shapes your lives with joy, freedom, and purpose.

I am deeply thankful for the **mentors** God has placed in my life—those who spoke truth when it was uncomfortable, extended grace when I was struggling, and modeled faith as relationship rather than performance. Your wisdom, example, and willingness to walk alongside me helped shape both my faith and my leadership.

To the **students and staff of John Melvin University**, thank you for allowing me to serve, lead, and grow alongside you. Your hunger for truth, purpose, and authentic faith continually reminds me why relationship—not religion—matters. Watching you pursue excellence while seeking Jesus has been both humbling and inspiring.

I am also grateful for my **ministry partners**—pastors, leaders, coaches, educators, and friends—who have shared this journey, prayed faithfully, and labored together in the work God has entrusted to us. Your partnership, encouragement, and commitment to people over platforms continue to reflect the heart of Christ.

Finally, to everyone reading this book: if you have ever struggled with faith, felt weighed down by religion, or longed for something deeper and more real, know that you are not alone. My prayer is that these pages point you—not to me, not to a system—but to the same relationship with Jesus that changed my life.

With deep gratitude,

David Angeron

A Spiritual Biography

"Abide in Me, and I in you. As the branch cannot bear fruit by itself, unless it abides in the vine, neither can you, unless you abide in Me." — John 15:4

This book is not a manual.

It is not a formula for spiritual success.

It is, in many ways, my spiritual biography.

I grew up surrounded by faith. I knew the stories. I understood the language. I could follow the structure. Faith was familiar to me. But familiarity is not intimacy.

As an athlete and later a coach and leader, I learned discipline, structure, and repetition. I trained relentlessly. I pursued excellence. Achievement became normal. Pressure became fuel. Momentum became identity.

Without realizing it, I approached God the same way.

I performed spiritually.

I maintained structure.

I preserved the image.

But beneath that discipline, something was missing.

Achievement can quietly mask spiritual distance. Religion can shape behavior while leaving the heart unchanged. Success can increase while intimacy decreases.

There came a season when pressure and misalignment exposed what routine religion could not repair. In that season, I didn't need more information about God—I needed connection. I needed honesty. I needed restoration.

What I discovered changed everything.

Real faith is formed in private.

Prayer is not performance.

Leadership flows from peace, not pressure.

Alignment with God matters more than adrenaline from accomplishment.

This book traces that shift—from knowing about Jesus to walking with Him daily. From striving to abiding. From image management to intimacy.

I share it not because my story is extraordinary, but because I believe it is common—especially among high achievers who win publicly while wrestling privately.

If this book does anything, I hope it gives you permission to be honest about your own journey. To evaluate whether your faith has become structured but distant. To rediscover the simplicity and power of private relationship with Christ.

This is not a finished story.

Spiritual biography is never finished. It unfolds daily through surrender, correction, trust, and grace. I am still learning. Still aligning. Still walking.

And that is the point.

"Come near to God and He will come near to you." — James 4:8

MORE THAN RELIGION

I didn't grow up lacking faith. In many ways, I grew up surrounded by it. Church wasn't foreign to me—it was familiar. I knew the stories long before I understood their depth. I knew the routines, the rhythms, the moments when to stand, when to sit, when to bow my head, and even which words would sound spiritual in the right setting. I knew about Jesus long before I ever truly knew Him. And for a long time, I honestly believed that was enough.

From the outside, it looked solid. I wasn't rebellious. I wasn't anti-faith. I was informed. I was present. I was engaged. But there is a massive difference between exposure and intimacy. There is a difference between being around something and being transformed by it. And I wouldn't understand that difference until much later.

As an athlete—and eventually as a coach—I learned something that cut straight through that illusion. Knowing the plays isn't the same as playing the game. Knowing the drills isn't the same as being in shape. Knowing the rules isn't the same as being transformed. That's true in sports. And it's profoundly true in faith.

You can study a playbook all day and still freeze under pressure. You can memorize strategy and still crumble when the lights come on. Information is powerful—but only when it moves from your head into your habits. Only when it shapes how you live.

Somewhere along the way, I had to confront a painful realization: my faith had become information without application. It sounded good. It looked right. But it wasn't shaping the core of who I was becoming.

As an athlete and later as a coach, I discovered a fundamental truth that applies on every field of life: information without application changes absolutely nothing. You can watch film all day, memorize every scheme, quote legendary coaches, and talk strategy with the best of them—but if it never makes its way onto the field, it's nothing more than noise. Empty noise.

And that's exactly what my faith had become.

Noise.

I had religion—but not relationship. I had routine—but not intimacy. I had knowledge—but not transformation. My spiritual life was something I carried around, not something that carried me. It was compartmentalized—separate from competition, separate from pressure, separate from ambition.

By the time I stepped into college athletics, faith already felt disconnected from my everyday reality. Church didn't seem to intersect with the weight of expectations, the temptations that came with performance culture, or the identity questions that quietly surface when wins and losses begin to define you. By my mid-twenties, coaching professional baseball, God had gradually moved to the periphery of my life. Not because I denied Him—but because I distracted myself from Him.

I was relentlessly pursuing success. Recognition. Security. Status. I trained my body with discipline. I sharpened my mind with intensity. I developed systems, strategies, and structures. But I was neglecting the one thing that mattered most—my soul.

What followed wasn't sudden. It was gradual. And it was inevitable.

Distance turned into drift.

Drift turned into compromise.

Compromise turned into collapse.

Collapse didn't come with flashing lights or headlines. It came with exhaustion. With emptiness. With the quiet realization that success had carried me somewhere I never intended to go. It was there—at rock bottom—that I finally grasped the truth no one had ever clearly taught me.

Christianity is not about trying harder.

It's about staying closer.

Jesus didn't come to build a religion centered on performance. He came to restore relationship. He didn't die so I could manage behavior better. He rose so I could walk with Him daily—honestly, imperfectly, but closely.

That revelation didn't just tweak my faith—it revolutionized my life. It changed how I lead. How I coach. How I parent. How I build teams. How I define success. How I respond to pressure. How I live when no one is watching. It shifted the foundation underneath everything.

This book is not a theological debate. It's not a checklist. It's not a performance plan dressed up as spirituality. It's a journey. A journey from empty religion to authentic relationship. From crushing pressure to liberating peace. From hollow outward success to genuine inward transformation. From merely knowing about Jesus to actually walking with Him.

If you're exhausted by performance-based faith… if you've drifted after being burned, distracted, or disappointed… if you love Jesus but feel distant from Him… if you're a high achiever who looks strong on the outside but feels empty on the inside… this book was written for you.

Because knowing about Jesus is not the same as knowing Him. And truly knowing Him changes absolutely everything.

Let's walk this path together.

I Trained for Everything— Except Relationship

I grew up immersed in religion. The routines, the stories, the expectations weren't just familiar—they were woven into the fabric of my childhood. Church shaped my schedule, my vocabulary, and even my understanding of what "good" looked like. It gave me structure. It gave me clarity. It gave me answers. I knew when to stand, when to sit, when to bow my head, and which responses would earn approval. From the outside, it looked solid. From the inside, it felt normal.

And for a long time, I believed mastering those patterns meant I was spiritually mature.

But here's the truth I came to understand—later than I wish I had: religion trained my behavior, but it never truly trained my heart for relationship. No one intentionally withheld that from me. It just wasn't emphasized. I was discipled in routine, not intimacy. I was taught the structure, not the connection. It was like being coached endlessly in drills but never being taught to love the game itself.

I learned the plays—but I never experienced the presence. I memorized the terminology—but I didn't know the Coach. I developed discipline—but not depth. And for years, I convinced myself that was enough.

I could quote Scripture. I could say the right things. I could blend in seamlessly. But looking prepared and being connected are two very different realities. You can wear the uniform without loving the game. You can study film without stepping onto the field. And deep down, I sensed something was missing.

I had trained for performance.

I had trained for approval.

I had trained for outcomes.

But I had never trained my heart for relationship.

When Faith Was Just Another Routine

As an athlete, routines weren't optional—they were essential. You train consistently. You condition past comfort. You show up whether you feel like it or not. You perform under pressure. Discipline becomes your language. It becomes identity.

So faith slid neatly into that same framework. Church became another scheduled commitment. Prayer became another obligation. Spiritual life became another routine to execute. Sunday attendance. Youth group midweek. Prayer before meals. It all fit into the rhythm—but it never reached my heart.

And here's what I learned the hard way: faith built only on routine will collapse under real pressure.

By the time I was 18 and playing college sports, church had become optional while practice was non-negotiable. Games were sacred. Training was required. Recovery and film study were priorities. Faith slowly drifted toward the margins—not because I stopped believing in God, but because I had never truly learned how to walk with Him personally.

There was no fire to protect. No intimacy to guard. No relationship to lose.

I didn't rebel loudly. I didn't storm away. I simply drifted.

And drifting is far more dangerous than rebellion.

Rebellion is visible. It forces confrontation. It demands a decision. Drifting is subtle. You miss one Sunday. Then another. You skip prayer once. Then a week. You get busy. You promise you'll reconnect later. And before you realize it, the distance feels normal.

That was my story.

I didn't wake up one morning and choose to abandon God. I replaced relationship with performance. I poured my identity into sports, into achievement, into measurable wins—because those gave immediate feedback. Scoreboards speak clearly. Faith, without intimacy, felt abstract.

When pressure increased—injuries, expectations, competition —I leaned on what I had trained most.

My body.

My mind.

My discipline.

But not my relationship with Christ.

If your faith is only routine, it won't survive adversity. Relationship is what anchors you when the scholarship changes, when the contract ends, when the injury lingers, or when the business deal falls through. Routine might shape behavior, but relationship sustains the soul.

Looking back, I see something clearly: God never drifted from me. I drifted because I had never built depth.

And that realization changed everything.

When Success Became the Only Scoreboard

By 26, I was coaching professional baseball. From the outside, it looked like arrival. I was living the dream many athletes chase. I was advancing quickly, gaining credibility, earning respect. I was in my element—on the field, in leadership, moving forward.

It felt like validation.

It felt like momentum.

It felt like winning.

And slowly— without realizing it—success became my scoreboard.

Faith wasn't rejected. It was sidelined. God wasn't attacked. He was postponed. I stopped asking spiritual questions and replaced them with performance-driven ones: How do I improve? How do I advance? How do I outwork everyone? How do I win at any cost?

That last question is the dangerous one.

When winning becomes your god, it never satisfies—it only demands.

It demands more time.

More energy.

More compromise.

More of your heart.

And eventually, more of your soul.

Materialism didn't crash into my life. It crept in quietly through comparison. Ego didn't explode. It expanded through praise. Control became my coping mechanism. Temptation normalized itself. Adultery trapped me. Anger fueled me. I managed public composure with discipline while internal chaos quietly multiplied.

On the outside, I was driven and focused. On the inside, I was fractured.

Disciplined—but hollow.

Successful—but disconnected.

Respected—but restless.

I trained my body relentlessly. I sharpened my mind strategically. I organized my schedule with excellence. But I neglected the one part of me that mattered most.

My soul wasn't injured. It was starved.

And when your soul is starved, no achievement can feed it.

Rock Bottom Isn't a Moment—It's a Collapse

By 35, everything I thought would sustain me had begun to unravel. The success. The identity. The control. The momentum. None of it could repair what was broken internally.

I knew how to endure pressure. I knew how to grind. I knew how to push through adversity. But I had never learned surrender. I had never learned how to let God lead instead of forcing outcomes myself.

Rock bottom didn't come with fireworks. It didn't announce itself dramatically. It came quietly—through exhaustion that sleep couldn't fix. Through shame that success couldn't hide. Through isolation that no crowd could erase.

It came as the painful realization that nothing external could repair what was broken inside.

That realization is terrifying. And freeing.

Because when everything collapses, you stop pretending.

And that's where God met me.

Not through routine.

Not through religion.

Not through performance.

Through relationship.

Authentic. Restorative. Life-giving relationship.

God didn't wait for me to improve my résumé. He didn't wait for flawless behavior. He met me in the wreckage. And what I feared would destroy me became the doorway to restoration.

I had trained for everything—except relationship.

But in that collapse, I finally began learning the one thing that would sustain me for the rest of my life.

Jesus Didn't Rescue Me—He Reclaimed Me

Here's what stunned me most in the middle of my collapse: God never demanded that I fix myself first. He didn't hand me a checklist. He didn't say, "Clean this up and then we'll talk." He didn't shame me into compliance or hold my failures over my head like leverage. Instead, He moved toward me. He reclaimed me.

That distinction matters deeply. Rescue can feel temporary—like pulling someone out of danger and sending them back on their own. Reclaiming is personal. It's intentional. It's relational. It says, "You are still Mine."

He met me in the wreckage of my own choices. When relationships were strained, when my reputation felt fragile, when shame was louder than hope—He remained steady. Faithful. Present. He didn't flinch at my mess. He didn't retreat from my weakness. He stepped closer.

And for the first time in my life, I stopped trying to impress God.

I started talking to Him.

Honestly.

Unfiltered.

Without performance.

Prayer stopped being scripted and polished. It became conversation. Scripture stopped being information I stored away for later. It became living revelation that shaped me daily. Obedience stopped feeling like forced compliance under a demanding authority. It became a loving response to grace that I didn't deserve.

Faith was no longer something I managed publicly. It became something I lived privately. That shift changed everything.

For the first time, I didn't just believe in Jesus—I walked with Him. Through setbacks. Through rebuilding. Through awkward growth. Through restoration that was beautiful but not instant. Not perfectly. Not polished. Not packaged for approval. But real.

Deeply real.

And that is what saved me—not success, not discipline, not reputation. Relationship.

Religion Taught Me Discipline—Relationship Taught Me Life

Religion taught me how to behave. Relationship taught me how to belong.

Religion gave me routines. Relationship gave me rest. Religion introduced me to stories about Jesus. Relationship taught me how to recognize His voice and respond when He speaks.

I still value discipline. I'll always be a coach at heart. I believe in structure. I believe in consistency. I believe in preparation, growth, and intentional habits. Discipline builds champions. Training matters. Structure creates stability.

But here's the truth I missed for years: you can train religiously every single day and still completely miss the heart of the game.

You can show up to church faithfully.

You can memorize Scripture.

You can serve with excellence.

You can look spiritually sharp on the outside.

And still never develop intimacy with Christ.

That realization humbled me in ways I didn't expect. Christianity was never about impressing a distant God with flawless execution. It was never about endless drills or spiritual perfection. It was always about walking with Him—daily, personally, honestly.

Relationship breathes life into discipline. It turns obedience into joy. It transforms routine into renewal.

Now when I pray, I'm not checking a box—I'm connecting with Someone who knows me fully. When I read Scripture, I'm not scanning for information—I'm listening for alignment. When I obey, it's not from pressure—it's from gratitude.

And here's the freedom I discovered: discipline without relationship drains you. Relationship fuels discipline. One exhausts. The other energizes. One is performance. The other is life.

That is the difference between religion and true intimacy with Christ.

Why This Book Exists

I'm writing this for the person who quietly sees themselves in my story.

For the athlete who trains relentlessly, performs at a high level, and carries discipline with pride—but feels empty when the lights turn off.

For the coach who builds winners, inspires excellence, and drives culture—but goes home exhausted in a way sleep can't fix.

For the leader who understands Scripture, teaches principles, and quotes verses—but feels distant from the very Author they proclaim.

For the believer who mastered religious habits but never experienced transformational intimacy.

If that's you, lean in close.

You are not broken beyond repair. You have not permanently disqualified yourself. You have not drifted too far. You haven't failed spiritually. You've simply been training the wrong way.

And here's the beautiful truth: Jesus is not standing at a distance waiting for your performance to improve. He's inviting you into relationship.

Not back into pressure.

Not back into perfectionism.

Not back into religious exhaustion.

But into something deeply personal.

The Relationship that restores identity.

The Relationship that rebuilds peace.

The Relationship that strengthens your calling instead of draining it.

This book isn't about creating better religious habits. It's about rediscovering the heart of your faith. And I promise you—from experience—when relationship is restored, everything changes.

Your leadership changes.

Your marriage changes.

Your focus sharpens.

Your joy returns.

Not because you try harder—but because you walk closer.

Reflection

When did faith slowly become routine instead of relationship for you? Was it when life got busy? When success demanded more time and energy? When disappointment quietly caused you to pull back? Or when pressure made performance feel safer than vulnerability?

What season are you currently training for right now? And what is it quietly costing your soul?

Every season extracts something. Every pursuit requires energy. The real question is this: is the cost producing life—or draining it?

Take a moment. Don't rush past this. The answer might reveal more than you expect.

Heart Check

Be honest with yourself.

Are you winning publicly while unraveling privately? Are you disciplined outwardly while disconnected inwardly? Are you leading others confidently while quietly feeling distant from God?

What would genuine surrender look like for you right now—not as weakness, but as courageous trust?

Surrender isn't quitting. It isn't abandoning ambition. It isn't stepping away from leadership or influence. It's releasing control. It's saying, "God, I've trained hard. Now lead me."

And sometimes the strongest move you can make isn't pushing harder—it's kneeling deeper.

Simple Prayer

Jesus, I've trained relentlessly for success. Now teach me how to walk with You. Not as a performance to impress others, but as a relationship that transforms me from the inside out. Rebuild what I've neglected. Restore what I've drifted from. Lead me—not just to achievement—but to life.

Amen.

CHAPTER 2

CHURCH DIDN'T FAIL ME— CONTROL DID

Let me say this clearly before we go any further: I believe in the Church. I attend a great church in Pensacola, FL. And I believe healthy church community is a gift—not an obstacle—to a thriving relationship with Jesus.

This book is not anti-church. But it is anti-control. It is anti-performance. And it is unapologetically honest about the damage that happens when religion quietly replaces relationship.

That distinction isn't small. It's essential to your spiritual freedom.

The Church, when healthy, is powerful. It's where believers gather, grow, serve, confess, heal, and worship together. It's where faith becomes lived out, not just discussed. Community matters. Accountability matters. Shepherding matters. Scripture calls us into fellowship for a reason—we were never designed to follow Jesus alone.

But control? Control suffocates.

Control confuses spiritual maturity with compliance. It elevates image over authenticity. It makes you feel managed instead of known. It measures behavior but never reaches the heart. And when faith becomes more about behavior management than heart transformation, something sacred is quietly lost.

Church didn't fail me.

But when performance creeps in and relationship fades out, damage begins.

And I want to be clear—this isn't about blame. It's about awareness. Because if we don't understand the difference between control and care, we risk rejecting the very gift God designed to strengthen us.

The Church is not the enemy. But control disguised as spirituality absolutely is. And when you can distinguish between the two, you protect both your faith and your freedom.

Why I Came Back to Church—The Right Way

When God pulled me out of the darkest season of my life, He didn't isolate me. He didn't say, "It's just you and Me from now on." He didn't lead me into spiritual independence that rejected community.

He led me back into it—but this time, into something healthy.

And it changed everything.

The church I attend now doesn't try to control my behavior. It doesn't pressure me to perform. It doesn't confuse loyalty to leadership with loyalty to Christ. Instead, it consistently strengthens my relationship with Jesus.

It points me back to Scripture—not opinion. It creates space for honesty—not perfection. It welcomes repentance—not reputation management. It encourages growth without demanding image.

That's what a healthy church does.

A good church reminds you that transformation takes time. A good church reminds you that grace is real, not theoretical. A good church reminds you that you don't walk alone—and that you don't have to pretend while you walk.

Here's the powerful truth I've learned: a healthy church doesn't compete with Jesus. It continually directs you to Him.

It doesn't replace relationship—it reinforces it.

It doesn't demand dependence—it builds maturity.

It doesn't shrink your faith—it strengthens it.

It equips you. It challenges you. It supports you. And then it gets out of the way so you can grow in Christ for yourself.

That's the kind of church I believe in. And that's the kind of church worth committing to with your whole heart.

Why Some People Walk Away (and Why I Get It)

When I walked away from church in my younger years, it wasn't rebellion—it was exhaustion.

I didn't feel spiritually strengthened. I felt spiritually managed. I didn't feel deeply known. I felt carefully measured.

And as an athlete and coach, I understand the difference between training that builds you and systems that break you.

Good coaching pushes you—but it also protects you. Good leadership challenges you—but it also develops you. It sees potential and builds capacity over time.

But unhealthy systems extract without restoring.

Some churches, often unintentionally, operate like high-pressure programs:

- No rest
- No margin
- No honest questions
- No room for growth
- No ownership in your own spiritual journey

Everything becomes about compliance. Everything becomes about maintaining image. Everything becomes about "don't mess this up."

That's not the Gospel. That's not Jesus.

Jesus didn't lead with fear. He didn't build loyalty through intimidation. He didn't silence questions—He answered them. He didn't crush the weary—He invited them to rest.

What pushes people away isn't Christ. It's control disguised as devotion.

And I understand why some walk away. I really do. If all you've experienced is pressure, measurement, and management, distance feels safer than performance. Silence feels safer than scrutiny. Independence feels safer than manipulation.

But here's the hope: just because you experienced unhealthy leadership doesn't mean you were meant to walk alone.

There is a difference between leaving control and leaving Christ.

Sometimes what feels like walking away from church is actually your soul crying out for something healthier—not something absent.

The answer isn't isolation. It's alignment.

Because healthy community doesn't suffocate your faith—it strengthens it. It doesn't replace relationship—it protects it. And when you find that kind of environment, growth no longer feels forced. It feels freeing.

That's where real healing begins. And that's where faith becomes strong enough to last.

The Difference Between a Church and a Religious Cult

This part matters—so read it slowly and carefully. Words like "church" get used in a lot of settings, but not every spiritual environment is healthy. Some places truly help you grow; others quietly train you to fear. And if you've ever felt confused, pressured, or spiritually trapped, I want to give you a clear lens—not to create suspicion, but to protect your freedom and sharpen your discernment.

A healthy church consistently points people to Jesus, not leaders. It encourages deep personal relationship with God and welcomes sincere questions without punishment. It builds people up into strong disciples, not dependent followers. It makes room for genuine rest, healthy boundaries, and growth at different paces, and it practices accountability with love and transparency. In contrast, a religious cult demands unwavering loyalty to leadership over Scripture. It discourages outside counsel and questioning, uses fear, shame, or isolation to control behavior, and makes people feel guilty for leaving—or even for resting. It positions leaders as untouchable spiritual gatekeepers and confuses obedience to God with submission to humans.

Here's the bottom line: a good church trains you to walk confidently with Jesus; a cult trains you to depend helplessly on the system. One produces lasting freedom. The other produces paralyzing fear. Jesus never asked for fear-based loyalty. He never said, "Follow Me or else." He invited people with love, truth, patience, and courage. He formed disciples by calling them—not by controlling them. If what you're experiencing feels like intimidation, manipulation, or pressure that keeps tightening instead of freeing, don't ignore it. God's voice may challenge you, but it will not enslave you.

Why Athletes and Leaders Are Especially Vulnerable

High performers are prime targets for religious control, and there's a reason for that. We're disciplined by nature. We respect authority. We're comfortable with structure. We're conditioned to push through pain. We're trained to do what it takes—no excuses. Those traits are powerful on the field and in leadership. But in an unhealthy spiritual environment, those same strengths can be used against you.

So when a system tells us, "Just trust us," "Don't question," "More sacrifice equals more spirituality," "Real leaders don't need rest," or "Your discomfort is proof you're growing," we often comply—even when our soul is quietly screaming in protest. That's the trap: athletes and leaders are used to pain being part of progress, so we assume that if it hurts, it must be working. But spiritual abuse doesn't produce maturity. It produces fear. It creates compliance, not transformation. It forms performers, not disciples.

Jesus is not a coach who breaks you to prove power. He's a Shepherd who strengthens you to build trust. He doesn't demand you ignore your conscience—He sharpens it. He doesn't silence your questions—He meets you in them. He doesn't confuse loyalty to a system with loyalty to Himself. If you're a leader, coach, or high achiever, hear me clearly: your discipline is a gift—but it must be guided by truth, not exploited by control.

Church as a Training Environment—not a Prison

The church I attend now understands a crucial truth: church should be a vibrant training ground, not a restrictive prison yard. A healthy church equips you for real life. It strengthens your faith muscles. It teaches you to think biblically, live courageously, love consistently, and walk with Jesus privately—not just look good publicly. It doesn't need you dependent on people; it wants you dependent on Christ.

Training builds lasting strength. It respects necessary recovery. It develops genuine maturity. It prepares you to live abundantly well, and over time it increases confidence and clarity. Prisons do the opposite. They restrict natural movement, enforce rigid compliance, suppress authentic identity, punish human weakness, and keep you fearful, exhausted, and small.

So here's a serious warning: if church makes you weaker spiritually—more anxious, more fearful, more ashamed, or more dependent on people instead of Christ—that's not just a red flag. That's a blaring alarm. Because the fruit matters. Healthy discipleship produces peace with courage. It produces conviction with compassion. It produces humility without humiliation. You should be growing in love, growing in freedom, growing in truth—becoming more like Jesus, not more afraid of humans.

And if your church environment feels like a cage, I want you to know this: Jesus didn't save you to imprison you. He saved you to restore you. And where the Spirit of the Lord is, there is freedom.

Jesus Never Replaced Relationship With Attendance

Let's be brutally honest for a moment: you can attend church every single week and still be distant from Jesus. You can serve faithfully, volunteer consistently, give generously—and still feel empty when you're alone. You can lead publicly and bleed privately. Attendance does not equal intimacy. Activity does not equal connection. Position does not equal transformation.

But here's the important distinction: while attendance doesn't guarantee intimacy, a healthy church powerfully supports it. Church should be a place where relationship is strengthened, Scripture is taught honestly and thoroughly, grace is practiced daily—not just preached—growth is encouraged rather than forced, and Jesus is always central. In a healthy church, you don't feel like a number;

you feel known. You aren't pressured to perform; you're invited to grow. You aren't shamed for struggling; you're supported through the process.

That's what I've found now, and that's why I'm still deeply committed to church. Not out of fear. Not out of image. Not out of pressure. But because healthy community sharpens my faith, strengthens my walk, and keeps Jesus at the center. Church didn't become less important when relationship became real—it became more meaningful, because now it flows from connection, not obligation.

If Church Has Hurt You

If you've been wounded by church, hear this from a coach who understands: you're not weak, you're not rebellious, and you're not broken. You were likely exposed to unhealthy leadership—not the true heart of Jesus. And that distinction matters.

Spiritual hurt cuts deep because it touches identity. It impacts trust. It makes you question what's safe. And sometimes the easiest response is to walk away from everything connected to the pain. But Jesus doesn't rush you past your wounds. He walks with you through them. He doesn't dismiss your experience, minimize your pain, or tell you to "just get over it."

Healing doesn't require isolation. It requires discernment. Isolation says, "I'll never trust again." Discernment says, "I'll learn what healthy looks like." Isolation may protect you temporarily, but discernment strengthens you permanently. You don't have to abandon your faith because someone misrepresented it. You don't have to walk away from Jesus because someone misused authority.

The goal isn't to harden your heart. It's to heal it—and rebuild it on truth.

The Goal Was Always the Same

Church was never meant to replace Jesus. It was designed to help you walk with Him. Religion says, "Submit or else." Relationship says, "Come walk with Me." Religion leans on fear. Relationship builds trust. Religion pressures conformity. Relationship cultivates transformation.

The invitation of Jesus has never changed. It's still personal. It's still gracious. It's still patient. He doesn't say, "Attend more." He says, "Abide in Me." He doesn't say, "Impress Me." He says, "Follow Me." That's the invitation that transformed my life, and it's the same invitation extended to you right now—no matter what your past experience has been.

Reflection

Does the church environment you're in genuinely strengthen your relationship with Jesus—or does it mainly manage your behavior? Be honest with yourself. Are you growing in freedom, clarity, and courage, or are you growing in anxiety, pressure, and fear? What fruit do you actually see right now—freedom or fear, peace or pressure, joy or obligation? The fruit always tells the truth, even when people try to explain it away.

Heart Check

Are you loyal to a system—or committed to Christ? Those are not always the same thing. What voices are shaping your faith most right now? Is it Scripture? Is it Jesus? Or is it personalities, pressure, and expectations? Healthy loyalty is rooted in truth. Unhealthy loyalty is rooted in fear. And only one of those produces life.

Simple Action Step

Pray honestly: "Jesus, show me what healthy spiritual community looks like for me." Then pay attention—not to hype, pressure, or charisma, but to peace. Peace doesn't mean perfection. It means alignment. And when you find an environment that strengthens your relationship with Christ instead of replacing it, you'll know—because freedom has a different feel than control. And once you experience that difference, you'll never settle for less again.

CHAPTER 3

CONTROL BREAKS WHAT FREEDOM BUILDS

One of the hardest lessons I had to learn—both in sports and in faith—is this powerful truth: control may create short-term compliance, but it quietly destroys long-term growth. I've seen this pattern play out more times than I can count. I've watched coaches control players into rigid obedience—only to lose their hearts. I've seen leaders demand submission while crushing the very confidence they were supposed to develop. I've observed systems that looked impressive on paper—wins, numbers, momentum, growth charts—but left people burned out, discouraged, and eventually gone.

And painfully, I've seen this same destructive pattern show up in religious environments.

From the outside, control can look productive. People fall in line. Standards are upheld. Order is maintained. But beneath the surface, something fragile is breaking. When fear becomes the primary motivator, freedom quietly disappears. And when freedom disappears, growth eventually stops. That's because freedom builds ownership, while control builds dependency. Freedom develops conviction, while control manufactures compliance. And only one of those produces lasting transformation.

If you've ever been in an environment where you felt like you had to constantly "be careful," constantly "get it right," constantly "stay in line," you know what I mean. It might look spiritual. It might even feel disciplined. But deep down, your soul can tell the difference between being formed and being managed.

Control Looks Like Discipline—Until It Isn't

Control is subtle. It rarely announces itself. It often disguises itself as discipline. At first, it sounds completely reasonable: "Hold the standard." "Demand excellence." "Don't let people slack off." "Keep everyone in line." As a coach, I understand standards. I believe in them. Excellence matters. Effort matters. Commitment matters. Discipline builds champions.

But there is a profound difference between discipline that develops and control that dominates.

Discipline builds trust. Control breeds fear. Discipline trains the heart. Control only manages behavior. Discipline says, "I believe in you." Control says, "I don't trust you." Discipline pushes you to grow stronger; control pushes you to stay smaller and dependent.

In healthy environments, discipline produces confidence. Athletes become self-led. Leaders grow in wisdom. Believers develop discernment. There's ownership. People don't just comply—they mature. They don't just follow—they learn to lead themselves well.

But under control, people stop thinking. They stop asking honest questions. They wait to be told what to do. They operate carefully, cautiously, and often anxiously. And here's the danger: both discipline and control can look intense from the outside. Both can use strong language. Both can hold high standards. Both can even produce short-term results.

But only one produces life.

The other produces quiet fear that eventually surfaces as rebellion, burnout, or collapse. That's why this matters—because you can build a system that looks strong while quietly breaking the people inside it.

What Control Does to the Soul

Control doesn't just shape behavior—it reshapes identity. Over time, it teaches subtle lies: "I'm only valued if I comply." "I'm only accepted if I perform." "I'm safe as long as I don't question." "If I mess up, I lose belonging." And when those lies take root, a person's relationship with God changes.

Instead of listening for His voice, they start listening for signals from the system. Instead of asking, "What is Jesus leading me to do?" they start asking, "What will get me in trouble?" "What will earn approval?" "What keeps me out of conflict?" That's not spiritual maturity. That's survival mode. Survival mode might keep you safe temporarily, but it will never produce deep, confident faith.

Jesus didn't form disciples who were afraid to speak. He formed disciples who were secure enough to step out, fail, learn, and grow.

He corrected them—but never controlled them. He challenged them—but never crushed their identity. Control shrinks the soul. Freedom strengthens it. Control makes you cautious. Freedom makes you courageous. Control keeps you dependent on humans. Freedom teaches you to depend on Christ.

And once you've experienced the difference, you can feel it immediately. Your soul knows when it's being managed, and your soul knows when it's being built. That's why this matters so much—because what control breaks, only freedom can rebuild. And Jesus has always been in the rebuilding business.

Jesus Never Used Control to Form Disciples

Look closely at how Jesus led His followers. He called—but He never coerced. He invited—but He never manipulated. He corrected—but He never humiliated. He challenged—but He never controlled. That leadership style should stop us in our tracks.

Jesus spoke with authority. He confronted sin. He raised the standard. But He never forced compliance. He never built loyalty through fear. He never tightened His grip when someone struggled. In fact, people walked away from Him—and remarkably, He let them go. He didn't chase them down to pressure them back. He didn't water down truth to keep them comfortable. He didn't threaten them into staying.

That one reality should reshape how we view spiritual leadership.

Control cannot tolerate freedom. Jesus requires it.

Freedom is not a side note in discipleship—it is the soil where real growth happens. Without freedom, love becomes obligation.

Without freedom, obedience becomes fear-driven. Without freedom, faith becomes fragile. Jesus didn't create followers who were trapped. He formed disciples who chose Him. And chosen love is always stronger than forced loyalty.

Freedom Is Risky—but It's the Only Way Growth Happens

As a coach, I learned this the hard way: you cannot develop leaders if you control their every decision. You cannot build maturity if you remove responsibility. You cannot expect ownership if you never release authority. Early in my coaching journey, I wanted everything tight—every drill precise, every decision filtered through me. It felt responsible. It felt strong. It felt "safe."

But it stunted growth.

Leadership develops when people are trusted. Freedom is risky—there's no way around that. People will fail. People will misread situations. People will make choices you wouldn't make. But without freedom, there can be no ownership. And without ownership, there can never be true maturity.

Jesus trusted His disciples with real responsibility—knowing full well they would stumble. Peter denied Him three times. Thomas doubted. All of them scattered in His darkest moment. Yet Jesus didn't rebuild them through tighter control. He restored them through relationship.

He met Peter with grace and a question: "Do you love Me?" He met Thomas with evidence and patience. He met the others with peace instead of condemnation. That's leadership anchored in confidence—not insecurity. Control tightens when afraid. Relationship strengthens when tested.

And Jesus was never afraid of their freedom.

Why Control Feels Spiritual (But Isn't)

Control appeals to fear—and fear can feel powerful. Fear gets fast results. Fear creates visible compliance. Fear makes people fall in line quickly. For a season, control-based systems can look impressive. Numbers may grow. Behavior may tighten. Public image may improve. On the outside, it can feel like momentum, strength, and "revival."

But transformation? That's another story.

Fear cannot produce a transformed heart. It can modify behavior. It can silence questions. It can enforce conformity. But it cannot create love. And without love, spiritual growth eventually collapses. That's why control-based religion often looks strong—until it doesn't. It builds an image instead of identity.

Underneath the polished surface, something fragile begins to fracture. People shrink internally. Joy quietly disappears. Honesty fades. Authenticity dies. Conversations become guarded. Questions become dangerous. Struggles become secrets. And eventually, people leave—not because they don't love Jesus, but because they cannot survive inside a system that suffocates the very freedom He offers.

Jesus never built faith on intimidation. He built it on invitation. He didn't scare people into loyalty; He loved them into transformation. And wherever freedom is missing, something essential is missing. Growth that lasts is never forced. It's formed—through truth, trust, and relationship.

Freedom Doesn't Mean Chaos

Here's where people often get it wrong: freedom is not disorder. Freedom is not lawlessness. Freedom is not "do whatever you want." Biblical freedom isn't reckless independence—it's responsibility with trust. It's the confidence to choose rightly without constant supervision. It's the strength to obey from conviction, not pressure. It's living aligned with truth because your heart has been transformed—not because someone is monitoring your behavior.

In the right church environment, under healthy leadership, within life-giving relationships, freedom produces authentic growth, spiritual discernment, genuine self-leadership, personal conviction, and true ownership. When people are trusted, they grow. When people are empowered, they mature. When people are guided by truth instead of gripped by fear, they develop internal strength that lasts beyond the environment that formed them.

That's why Paul declared so clearly, "It is for freedom that Christ has set us free." Not for control. Not for fear. Not for manipulation. But for true, life-giving freedom. Freedom doesn't remove standards—it internalizes them. Freedom doesn't eliminate accountability—it makes it relational instead of rigid. And when freedom is understood correctly, it doesn't produce chaos. It produces character.

Why Leaders Must Be Careful

Control almost always grows from insecurity. Insecure leaders fear losing influence. Insecure systems fear honest questions. Insecure churches fear independent thinkers. When identity is fragile, control feels protective—but it's destructive.

Healthy leaders don't fear questions; they welcome them. They understand that truth doesn't collapse under scrutiny. If anything, it becomes clearer. Healthy churches don't demand loyalty—they inspire trust. Healthy leadership says, "Let's search Scripture together." "Let's talk through your concerns." "Let's grow in discernment." Control says, "Don't question." "Just submit." "Trust us, not your conscience."

If a system cannot survive honest conversation, it isn't built on truth—it's built on control. And that distinction makes all the difference in spiritual formation. Maturity grows in environments where thinking is encouraged, not suppressed. When leaders are secure in Christ, they don't need to micromanage people. They can guide without gripping. They can correct without crushing. They can release without fearing abandonment. And that kind of leadership produces strength—not dependency.

Freedom Builds What Control Never Can

Control may hold people together temporarily, but freedom builds people who can stand on their own. Control creates followers; freedom develops sons and daughters. Control keeps people physically close; freedom keeps people relationally connected.

There's a powerful difference between someone staying because they're afraid and someone staying because they trust. Jesus didn't die to give us religious supervision—He died to restore family. He didn't form disciples to monitor them. He formed them to send them.

When you understand that, everything changes. You stop asking, "How do I avoid getting in trouble?" and you start asking, "How do I grow into who God created me to be?" Control shrinks vision. Freedom expands it. Control limits identity. Freedom clarifies it.

This truth reshapes how we approach church, leadership, discipleship—even parenting and coaching. Because what control can never manufacture, freedom can cultivate: confidence, conviction, courage, and love. And at the end of the day, that's what Jesus builds—people who are strong enough to stand, humble enough to follow, and free enough to truly love.

What Freedom With Jesus Feels Like

Freedom with Jesus feels lighter—yet somehow stronger at the same time. It feels clear, but never forced. It feels challenging, but deeply safe. There is conviction—but not condemnation. There is growth—but not grinding pressure.

Freedom says, "I choose obedience—not because I'm afraid, but because I trust Him." That's a completely different motivation. Fear says, "If I don't, I'll lose." Trust says, "If I do, I'll grow." Freedom confidently affirms, "I can hear God for myself." "I can grow at an honest pace." "I can ask real questions." "I can fail—and still be completely loved."

That last one changed everything for me. When you know you are secure, you stop hiding. When you stop hiding, you start healing. And when you start healing, real transformation begins. Freedom creates an atmosphere where growth is sustainable. You don't burn out trying to maintain image. You don't exhaust yourself trying to earn belonging. You don't panic every time you stumble.

You learn. You repent. You adjust. You keep walking.

That's the environment where disciples are formed—not controlled, not pressured, not micromanaged—but strengthened. And that is where real, lasting change happens.

The Question That Reveals Everything

Here's a simple but powerful diagnostic question: does your faith environment operate more on fear—or trust? Sit with that. Fear-based systems tighten control. They increase monitoring. They discourage questioning. They imply that proximity equals safety. Trust-based relationships release responsibility. They encourage discernment. They strengthen personal conviction. They allow room to grow.

Jesus consistently chose trust. He entrusted disciples with assignments. He entrusted them with authority. He entrusted them with the message—even after they failed. He didn't hover. He didn't micromanage. He didn't revoke calling at the first mistake. And He's still inviting us into that kind of freedom today.

Freedom doesn't mean there are no standards. It means the standard is written on the heart—not enforced by fear. And that difference reveals everything.

Reflection

Where in your life have you experienced control disguised as spirituality? Was it subtle or obvious? Did it feel intense or quietly draining? How did it affect your relationship with God? Did you grow closer to Him—or more anxious around Him? Did you feel empowered—or constantly evaluated?

Take time to consider how those experiences shaped your understanding of spiritual authority. Awareness is not bitterness— it's clarity. And clarity creates the opportunity for healing.

Heart Check

Right now, do you feel trusted—or merely managed? Are you growing in confidence before God—or constantly worried about disappointing people? What emotion most consistently dominates your faith journey: peace or pressure, joy or anxiety, confidence or constant second-guessing?

Healthy faith should stretch you—but it should not suffocate you. It should convict you—but not crush you. It should guide you—but not grip you.

Simple Action Step

Ask Jesus directly, "Where am I obeying out of fear instead of trust?" Sit with that question. Listen carefully—not for accusation, but for invitation. His voice does not shame. His voice does not panic. His voice does not threaten. He leads with clarity and kindness.

And when obedience flows from trust instead of fear, faith stops feeling heavy. It starts feeling alive. And that is the kind of freedom Jesus died to restore.

CHAPTER 4

WHY COMPETITORS AND HIGH ACHIEVERS STRUGGLE SPIRITUALLY

Competitors and high achievers are trained to win. It's embedded in our DNA—woven into how we think, how we plan, how we measure life. We are wired to chase standards, track progress, grind through adversity, and push past limits that would stop most people cold. We don't just like goals—we need them. We measure everything. We optimize everything. We compete with ourselves when no one else is watching.

That mindset builds championships. It builds companies. It builds reputations. It builds movements.

But spiritually, that same wiring can quietly work against us.

Because in faith, the scoreboard looks different.

If we're not careful, we carry our performance mindset into our relationship with God and slowly create distance between our achievements and our souls. Success grows. Platforms expand. Influence increases. But intimacy shrinks. And the gap widens with every win that isn't rooted in presence.

The Strength That Wins Games Can Strain the Soul

As an athlete—and later as a coach—I mastered physical training. I sharpened mental focus. I learned how to outwork competition. I understood how to push through pain when others tapped out. Pressure fueled me. Deadlines sharpened me. Expectations elevated me.

But what no one really showed me was how to rest my soul.

Religion gave me routines. Faith environments gave me rules. But I never learned how to slow down and simply know Jesus. And that distinction matters more than we realize.

High achievers excel at doing. But relationship with Jesus is rooted in being.

Being known.

Being loved.

Being still.

Being secure—without proving anything.

That's unfamiliar territory for driven leaders. We've been rewarded our entire lives for output. Train harder. Study longer. Prepare more. Outwork everyone. But you cannot grind your way into intimacy with God. You cannot hustle your way into peace.

And when we try, something begins to strain. The very strength that wins games—the capacity to push, grind, and perform—can quietly exhaust the soul when applied to faith. Because the Kingdom doesn't run on hustle. It runs on trust. And trust requires surrender, not stamina.

We Were Trained to Earn—Not Receive

High achievers live by scoreboards. Stats. Results. Wins. Losses. Rankings. Benchmarks. We're conditioned to measure progress. So when we step into faith, we naturally start asking, "How am I doing?" "Am I growing fast enough?" "Am I disciplined enough?" "Am I reading enough?" "Am I good enough?"

Without realizing it, we turn grace into a performance metric.

We track prayer like reps.

We track Scripture like stats.

We evaluate growth like a season record.

We don't mean to do it. It's just how we've succeeded everywhere else.

Religion feeds that instinct. Do more. Try harder. Stay consistent. Don't mess up. Relationship confronts it—because grace cannot be earned. And that unsettles achievers. We are comfortable earning. We are uncomfortable receiving. We understand performance. We struggle with unconditional love.

But here is the freeing truth: grace levels the scoreboard. You cannot outperform your way into more love from God. You cannot hustle your way into deeper worth. You cannot achieve your way into acceptance.

You start accepted.

You begin loved.

You move forward from belonging—not toward it.

That shift—from earning to receiving—is where high achievers either deepen their faith or exhaust themselves trying to win something that was already given.

You don't have to win with Jesus. You get to walk with Him. And walking is very different from performing.

Why Religion Feels Familiar to High Performers

Religion makes sense to achievers. It fits our wiring. It provides structure, expectations, and measurable effort. Show up. Read more. Serve more. Try harder. Do better. That feels like training—and training is our comfort zone.

We understand repetition. We understand accountability. We understand targets and metrics. Give us a checklist and we will execute it. Give us a standard and we will chase it.

But Jesus never offered a spiritual performance plan. He offered Himself.

That's the tension.

High achievers often replace intimacy with intensity. We confuse discipline with devotion. We chase improvement instead of presence. We treat prayer like reps instead of relationship. Intensity feels spiritual—but intensity alone doesn't equal intimacy.

You can be highly disciplined and emotionally distant. You can be spiritually active and relationally disconnected. Eventually something gives. Either burnout hits because we're trying to outwork a relationship—or drift sets in because we secretly feel like we're failing at faith.

The truth is humbling: we approached it like a performance arena instead of a relationship.

My Own Drift as an Athlete and Coach

By the time I reached college athletics, church felt like background noise in my achievement-driven life. I knew the stories. I knew the verses. I knew the language. But I didn't know Jesus personally. So I slowly stopped showing up—not in rebellion, but in distraction.

My schedule filled up. My goals expanded. My ambitions sharpened. There were games to win, rosters to manage, reputations to build. Life became measured by tangible results and visible progress. Church felt less urgent because it didn't feel measurable.

By my mid-twenties, coaching professional baseball, God and church had quietly disappeared from my priorities. I was chasing success, respect, financial security, and validation with relentless focus. I called it drive. I called it commitment. I called it excellence.

In reality, I was empty—and didn't know it.

Achievement masked the distance for a while. Winning feels good. Recognition fills the ego. Advancement distracts the heart. Success can temporarily numb spiritual drift. But eventually the noise fades. The locker room empties. The crowd disappears. The deals close.

And you're left alone with what you've built.

If there's no depth beneath it, you feel it. The void doesn't announce itself loudly—it whispers. A quiet restlessness. A subtle dissatisfaction. A question you can't shake: Is this all there is?

And that whisper, if you listen closely enough, is often the beginning of return.

Why High Achievers Hide Spiritually

High achievers hate weakness. We don't like not having answers. We don't like asking for help. We don't like admitting confusion. And we certainly don't like slowing down long enough to feel something uncomfortable. Weakness feels like vulnerability, and vulnerability feels like exposure.

So spiritually, we adapt.

We hide doubt behind confident language. We bury exhaustion beneath more activity. We mask emptiness with achievement. We lead. We serve. We grind. But we don't rest—and we don't receive.

We would rather fix ourselves than surrender. We would rather improve than admit need. We would rather perform than confess weakness. But here's the paradox that changed my life: Jesus does not avoid weakness—He invites it. Not to shame it, but to redeem it.

"Bring Me your burden."

"Bring Me your doubt."

"Bring Me your exhaustion."

Achievers see weakness as the enemy of excellence. Jesus sees it as the starting line of grace. Because when you stop pretending to be strong, you finally become honest. And honesty is where real intimacy begins.

You cannot build relationship while hiding. You cannot receive grace while posturing strength. Sometimes the strongest move a high achiever can make is not pushing harder—but kneeling deeper. That isn't quitting. That's surrender. And surrender isn't weakness—it's trust. And trust is where your soul finally finds rest.

Jesus Challenged High Performers Differently

Jesus didn't struggle with broken people. He struggled with accomplished ones. The Pharisees knew Scripture inside and out. They followed rules meticulously. They hit spiritual metrics with precision. From the outside, they looked spiritually elite. But they missed Him completely.

Why? Because achievement often produces self-reliance. And self-reliance, left unchecked, suffocates relationship.

Broken people knew they needed help. High performers often believed they had it handled. So Jesus challenged them differently. He didn't say, "Try harder." He said, "Come follow Me." He didn't say, "Impress Me." He said, "Lay it down." He didn't say, "Optimize your effort." He said, "Abide." He didn't say, "Prove your commitment." He said, "Rest." He didn't say, "Earn this." He said, "Receive."

To achievers, that language sounds passive. Abide. Rest. Receive. It doesn't sound intense or competitive. But those are not weak commands—they are deeply powerful ones. Abiding requires trust. Rest requires surrender. Receiving requires humility. And humility is often the hardest lesson for the accomplished.

Jesus wasn't trying to slow high performers down. He was trying to set them free from the pressure of performing for God instead of walking with Him.

Why High Achievement Can Delay Surrender

High achievers don't hit rock bottom easily. We are wired to solve problems. When pressure rises, we adjust. When doors close, we pivot. When obstacles appear, we push harder. That resilience is a gift—but spiritually, it can delay surrender.

Instead of surrendering, we optimize. Instead of repenting, we re-strategize. Instead of confessing weakness, we double down on effort. Instead of resting, we grind more intensely.

That was me.

If something wasn't working, I didn't pause—I pushed. If something felt off, I didn't surrender—I fixed. That approach works in business. It works in athletics. It works in leadership. But it doesn't work with God.

You cannot out-strategize spiritual emptiness. You cannot outwork distance from Him. You cannot problem-solve your way into intimacy.

For me, it took collapse—not coaching. It took brokenness—not discipline. It took rock bottom—not motivation. Only when every strategy failed did I finally learn the transformative power of relationship.

Surrender isn't what achievers default to. But it is what our souls desperately need.

What Changes When Achievers Learn Relationship

When high achievers finally encounter genuine relationship with Jesus, everything shifts—not slightly, but completely.

Obedience becomes alignment, not pressure. Prayer becomes honesty, not performance. Rest becomes strength, not weakness. Grace becomes fuel, not a threat to excellence.

We stop trying to prove ourselves and start walking securely. We stop measuring spiritual growth like a stat sheet and start cultivating closeness. We stop asking, "How am I doing?" and begin asking a better question: "Am I close?"

That single question changes everything.

When you're close, obedience flows naturally. When you're close, conviction feels clear—not condemning. When you're close, growth becomes steady—not frantic.

High achievers don't lose their drive when they discover relationship. Their drive gets purified. It becomes anchored. Healthy. Sustainable. You still pursue excellence—but from identity, not insecurity. You still lead—but from humility, not ego. You still work hard—but not to earn love.

Relationship doesn't diminish ambition. It redeems it.

Jesus Doesn't Compete With Your Drive—He Redeems It

Jesus isn't anti-discipline. He's anti-self-salvation. He doesn't erase ambition—He reorders it. He doesn't remove intensity—He anchors it in love.

Drive is not the enemy. Self-reliance is. Ambition isn't the problem. Identity confusion is.

When achievers finally discover authentic relationship with Jesus, something powerful happens. Their drive matures. It becomes steady instead of frantic. Purposeful instead of pressured. Eternal instead of ego-driven.

They stop performing for approval and start operating from identity.

They still prepare.

They still pursue excellence.

They still compete.

But now their effort flows from being secure—not striving to secure. And when identity is unshakable, effort becomes joyful instead of exhausting. That is where redeemed ambition lives.

The Invitation to High Achievers

Jesus isn't asking you to stop striving overnight. He's asking you to stop striving alone. He isn't lowering your standards. He's inviting you to shift the source of your strength.

From earning → receiving.

From grinding → abiding.

From proving → trusting.

From pressure → peace.

That transition feels uncomfortable at first. It feels slower. Less measurable. Less controllable. And achievers don't love what they can't measure. But this is where real freedom begins—freedom no championship ring can provide, no financial milestone can secure, and no title can sustain.

You don't have to become less driven. You just have to become more connected. And when connection becomes the priority, everything else finds its proper place.

Reflection

Where has your drive genuinely helped your faith? Maybe it kept you disciplined. Maybe it kept you consistent when others drifted. Acknowledge that.

Now ask the harder question: Where has that same drive quietly hindered intimacy with the God who created you for relationship— not just results?

Have you rushed through prayer just to complete it?

Have you treated Scripture like a checklist?

Have you measured spiritual growth like performance data?

Awareness isn't condemnation. It's clarity. And clarity positions you to grow.

Heart Check

Are you trying to master faith the way you mastered your sport? Are you training for spiritual success—or learning to remain close to Jesus?

One builds performance. The other builds relationship.

Are you constantly evaluating yourself…

Or simply walking with Him?

The greatest strength you can develop spiritually isn't perfection. It's proximity. And proximity changes everything.

Simple Action Step

This week, pause before one routine spiritual discipline. Before you open Scripture. Before you bow your head. Before you walk into church. Ask yourself honestly:

"Am I doing this to perform—or to be present?"

Don't rush past that question. Let it settle. Then invite Jesus into that moment of honesty. No pressure. No pretending. No spiritual posing. Just presence.

That small shift—from performance to presence—may feel simple. But it could mark the beginning of the relationship you've been searching for all along.

Because the goal was never mastery.

It was closeness.

And closeness changes everything.

CHAPTER 5

WHEN WINNING ISN'T ENOUGH

There comes a defining moment in every competitor's life when winning no longer satisfies the soul. Not because the passion has faded. Not because the effort has weakened. But because the scoreboard cannot reach the emptiness underneath.

I know that moment intimately.

For years, achievement kept me comfortably numb. As an athlete—and later as a professional baseball coach—the wins gave me temporary highs. The grind gave me direction. The chase delivered adrenaline that felt like purpose. Success became my identity—something visible I could point to and confidently say, "See—this is who I am." It was measurable. It was celebrated. It was applauded.

But slowly—almost unnoticed—something inside me began to erode.

The celebration windows grew shorter. The satisfaction evaporated faster. The next goal appeared sooner. The joy didn't last as long. The silence afterward felt louder. The wins had to get bigger just to feel the same. Winning worked—until suddenly, painfully, it didn't.

That realization is unsettling for a competitor. Because if winning doesn't fill you... what will? And that question, as uncomfortable as it is, becomes the doorway to something deeper than achievement ever offered.

Success Can Distract You From Emptiness

High performers rarely collapse overnight. We compensate. When something feels off internally, we don't slow down—we accelerate. When the soul aches, we increase output. When peace feels distant, we push harder. When uncertainty creeps in, we create more goals.

We are masters at staying productive.

Success becomes spiritual anesthesia. It dulls discomfort. It masks questions. It delays reckoning. I didn't drift from God because I rejected Him. I drifted because I was busy—busy building programs, busy developing players, busy chasing titles, busy managing responsibilities.

By my mid-20s, church wasn't offensive—it was irrelevant. God wasn't denied—He was overlooked. Not out of anger, but distraction. And distraction is more dangerous than rebellion because it doesn't feel dramatic. It feels responsible. Strategic. Driven.

You tell yourself, "I'll reconnect when things slow down." But things rarely slow down. Success doesn't eliminate emptiness—it postpones confronting it. And postponement has an expiration date. Eventually, the noise fades, the calendar clears for a moment, and what you've been avoiding starts whispering louder than any applause ever did.

Achievement Makes a Poor Savior

Achievement promises identity. But it cannot deliver lasting significance.

Wins fade. Titles expire. Roles evolve. Seasons end. Crowds move on. And when your identity is tied to performance, every loss becomes personal. Every setback shakes you. Every failure threatens you. Every critique feels like exposure.

I didn't realize how deeply I depended on achievement until it stopped filling me. That's when frustration turned into anger. Ambition shifted into obsession. Discipline hardened into control. And control slowly led into darkness.

What started as hunger for excellence gradually became hunger for more—more recognition, more affirmation, more applause, more escape. The more I accomplished, the more I needed. Achievement didn't save me. It exposed me. It revealed that what looked like confidence was often insecurity in disguise.

Achievement is a tool. It is a gift. But it was never meant to be a savior. Because a scoreboard can measure performance—but it cannot define purpose. And when you finally realize that winning isn't enough, you are not standing in defeat. You are standing at the edge of awakening.

The Dark Season No One Sees on Social Media

By my early 30s, from the outside, my life didn't look broken. It looked successful. The career was strong. The reputation was intact. Leadership opportunities were expanding. If you scrolled through the highlights, everything appeared impressive.

But internally, I was fighting battles no one could see.

Temptation wasn't occasional—it was constant. Compromise wasn't rare—it became routine. Anger wasn't a flare-up—it became my emotional baseline. Sin wasn't something I resisted—it was something I carefully justified.

And the most dangerous part? I was fully functional.

Still coaching effectively. Still leading teams. Still achieving results. Still smiling publicly.

But spiritually, I was distant. Far from God. Far from peace. Far from the version of myself I knew I was created to be.

Religion had trained me to look polished. It taught me language, appearance, and how to manage perception. But it never taught me how to come home—to be honest, vulnerable, and fully seen. When you're high-functioning but hollow, it can go unnoticed for years. Until it can't.

Rock Bottom Is a Mercy in Disguise

Rock bottom doesn't always arrive with public scandal or dramatic headlines. Sometimes it comes quietly—through exhaustion that sleep can't fix, through success that no longer satisfies, through a growing awareness that something inside is unraveling.

At 35, I didn't just hit failure. I hit emptiness.

The grind stopped working. The wins stopped numbing. The escapes stopped satisfying. The buried anger stopped staying buried. For the first time in years, I didn't need strategy. I didn't need motivation. I didn't need a better plan.

I needed rescue.

And here's what I've learned: rock bottom can be mercy in disguise. Because when everything else collapses, you finally stop pretending you're fine. You stop managing image. You stop spinning narratives. You stop optimizing broken systems.

That's exactly where Jesus met me.

Not with a lecture. Not with condemnation. Not with a religious checklist. But with steady, unwavering presence.

Rock bottom didn't destroy me. It exposed the illusion that I could save myself. And that exposure became the doorway to healing.

Jesus Didn't Fix Me—He Found Me

When I finally encountered Jesus in that season, something shifted deeply. He didn't "fix" me like a project. He found me.

I didn't suddenly become more disciplined. I became dependent. I didn't instantly clean everything up. I stopped pretending I had it together. I didn't adopt another system. I entered relationship.

For the first time, faith wasn't about routines or rules. It was about surrender—honest, uncomfortable, freeing surrender. It was saying, "I don't have this handled. I can't grind my way out. I need You."

And instead of pulling away, Jesus leaned in.

He didn't require explanations. He didn't demand I defend myself. He didn't stand over me in disappointment. He invited me to walk with Him—one step, one day, one honest conversation at a time.

That shift—from performance to presence—changed everything. Because when you're found, you stop running. When you're accepted, you stop hiding. And when you finally experience relationship—not religion—it doesn't just adjust your behavior.

It transforms your heart.

And that transformation is what success could never deliver.

Why Winning Without Jesus Leaves You Empty

Winning without Jesus forces you to carry weight you were never created to hold. Identity. Worth. Meaning. Legacy. Those aren't trophies you display—they're burdens you feel. And they are crushing when you try to carry them alone.

When success becomes your source, every win has to mean more. Every achievement has to answer deeper questions: *Who am I? Why do I matter? What will last when the lights go out?* That's too much pressure for a scoreboard. Too much responsibility for a title. Too much expectation for applause.

Only Jesus can hold those questions without them collapsing you.

When relationship with Him became real for me—when it moved from routine to personal—everything shifted. Success stopped being my source; it became stewardship. Coaching stopped defining who I was; it became a calling. Achievement stopped being my god; it became a tool.

And tools are powerful—when they're in the right hands.

But when you try to build your identity on them, they eventually crack under the weight. Winning is a gift. Excellence is honorable. Pursuing greatness is not the problem. The problem is asking a win to tell you who you are.

Victory was never meant to be your foundation. Jesus is.

The Freedom of Not Needing the Win

The greatest freedom I experienced wasn't just forgiveness.

It was rest.

Rest from constant proving. Rest from performing for approval. Rest from chasing validation that always seemed just out of reach.

For years, every win validated me—and every loss threatened me. If we won, I felt secure. If we lost, I felt exposed. My emotional stability rose and fell with the outcome of the season. That's a heavy way to live.

But in relationship with Jesus, something remarkable happened: I could lose—without losing myself. I could win—without worshiping the victory. I could lead—without needing applause to confirm my value.

That kind of freedom changes how you compete.

You still prepare. You still pursue excellence. You still want to win. But you no longer need the win to breathe. You're anchored deeper than outcomes. And that anchor steadies you when the season shifts, when titles change, when platforms fade.

Genuine relationship doesn't dull your competitiveness. It purifies it. Because when your identity is secure, competition becomes expression—not desperation. Effort becomes gratitude—not grasping. And that is real freedom.

Church Matters—But Only the Right Kind

Today, I'm part of a vibrant church community. And I believe deeply that church matters. Community matters. Worship matters. Accountability matters. We were never designed to walk alone.

But not every church strengthens relationship. Some—often unintentionally—replace it.

That distinction is crucial.

A truly healthy church:

- Consistently points you toward Jesus—not personalities
- Strengthens your personal relationship with God—without fostering unhealthy dependence
- Welcomes honest questions—without manipulation or control
- Produces freedom—never fear

A religious cult controls access to God. A healthy church clears obstacles from the path to Him. One tightens its grip. The other releases you to grow.

I didn't need less church. I needed the right church—the kind that fuels relationship, reinforces Scripture, and encourages growth at a healthy pace. Church was never meant to compete with Jesus. It was meant to walk alongside you as you walk with Him.

And when you find that kind of community, something powerful happens. You grow stronger. You grow freer. You grow deeper in the only relationship that truly sustains you.

What Changed When Relationship Became Central

I stopped obsessively asking, "How am I performing spiritually? Am I consistent enough? Disciplined enough? Doing enough?" And I started asking the only question that truly matters: *Am I genuinely close to Jesus?*

That shift sounds small. It isn't. It recalibrated everything.

When performance stopped being the focus and presence became the goal, every area of my life began to realign. Marriage shifted—from expectation to connection. Fatherhood shifted—from pressure to presence. Coaching shifted—from ego to impact. Leadership shifted—from control to stewardship. Faith shifted—from routine to relationship.

I stopped chasing perfection. I started pursuing presence.

And presence produces something performance never can: peace. Not passive peace. Not complacent peace. A steady, anchored peace that holds under pressure.

When closeness becomes the goal, growth becomes natural. Conviction becomes clear. Correction becomes constructive.

You're no longer trying to "ace" Christianity—you're walking with Christ. And walking changes the rhythm of everything.

Still Learning How to Walk

Relationship didn't make me flawless. It made me honest—courageously honest.

I no longer have to pretend I've mastered anything. I don't need to posture strength or hide weakness. I can bring doubt, frustration, temptation, and fatigue directly to Him.

Relationship didn't remove discipline. It gave discipline direction.

Now when I pray, it's not to check a box—it's to connect. When I open Scripture, it's not to complete a task—it's to listen. When I correct myself, it's not from shame—it's from conviction rooted in love.

Relationship didn't dull my competitive edge. It redeemed it. It grounded my intensity in something lasting. It anchored my drive in identity instead of insecurity. I still strive for excellence—but I no longer strive for approval.

And I'm still walking.

Still learning. Still growing. Still returning when I drift.

But now I walk with a confidence I never had before—not confidence in my discipline, not confidence in my consistency, but confidence that I'm not alone.

And that changes everything about how you move forward.

Reflection

What have you been asking achievement to give you that only Jesus can provide? Security? Validation? Peace? Purpose?

Be honest.

Where have you expected a scoreboard, a title, a platform, or a paycheck to fill something spiritual?

Awareness is powerful. Because once you identify what you've been chasing, you can redirect it toward something eternal.

Heart Check

If everything external disappeared tomorrow—the title, the recognition, the success, the position—would your core identity still stand?

Would you still know who you are?

Relationship with Jesus builds identity that survives loss. Performance-based identity collapses when outcomes shift.

Which foundation are you standing on right now?

Simple Action Step

This week, tell Jesus honestly where winning hasn't been enough.

Don't clean it up. Don't spiritualize it. Don't try to solve it first.

Just say it.

"Jesus, this didn't satisfy me."

"This didn't fix what I thought it would."

"I'm more tired than I admit."

Bring your raw truth to Him. Then pause. Don't rush to the next task. Don't move into problem-solving mode.

Just sit in His presence.

Because relationship doesn't begin with performance. It begins with honesty.

And honesty is where freedom takes root.

CHAPTER 6

REBUILDING FAITH AFTER COLLAPSE

Collapse has a sound to it.

It's not always loud. It doesn't always make headlines. Sometimes it's quiet—a slow internal crack that finally gives way.

For me, collapse didn't look dramatic on the outside. There was no public disgrace. No viral moment. No visible implosion. It looked like exhaustion. It felt like emptiness. It sounded like the quiet realization that I had been sprinting with intensity—but in the wrong direction—for far too long.

Every athlete understands this: you cannot rebuild strength until you acknowledge injury. Denial delays healing. You can tape it up. You can push through. You can convince yourself it's just soreness. But eventually, what you ignore will sideline you.

Spiritually, I wasn't slightly strained. I wasn't mildly fatigued. I was deeply wounded. Disconnected from peace. Disconnected from clarity. Disconnected from God.

And until I admitted that, nothing could change.

That admission wasn't dramatic. It was quiet. It was personal. It was humbling. But it was the turning point. Because healing doesn't begin when you impress people with strength—it begins when you tell the truth about weakness.

Collapse Is Not the End—It's the Diagnosis

When everything crumbled internally, I honestly expected instant repair. I thought God would rush in, sweep away the debris, restore momentum, and put me back on the field stronger overnight.

But that's not how real healing works.

Not in sports. Not in life. Not in faith.

You don't tear a ligament and walk it off the next day. You diagnose it. You sit with it. You treat it. You rebuild slowly. You follow the process even when it feels frustratingly gradual.

Collapse wasn't God rejecting me. It was God getting my attention.

And sometimes the most loving thing God can allow is the collapse of the illusion that we're fine.

I didn't lose my faith at rock bottom. I lost the illusion that I could manage faith on my own. That illusion is especially dangerous for achievers. We think we can optimize everything—including our spirituality. We assume discipline and strategy can substitute for surrender.

But faith isn't managed. It's surrendered.

Collapse stripped me of the belief that I could self-correct without Him. And that stripping felt painful—but it was precise. It wasn't destruction. It was diagnosis. And diagnosis is the first step toward real healing.

You Don't Rehab by Pretending You're Fine

In athletics, the worst mistake an injured player can make is hiding it. You compensate. You favor one side. You push through discomfort. You tell yourself it's manageable. And eventually, you make it worse.

That's exactly what I had done spiritually.

I performed injured. I showed up. I functioned. I led. I achieved. But I was compensating the entire time. I leaned on charisma instead of character. On structure instead of surrender. On results instead of relationship.

Religion gave me the tools to look strong. Jesus gave me the courage to admit I wasn't.

Rebuilding faith didn't start with powerful sermons or polished prayers. It started with confession—not public, not dramatic, just real.

"God, I don't trust myself."

"God, I've made a mess."

"God, I don't even know how to come back."

That wasn't weakness. That was honesty.

And honesty is where healing begins.

You don't rehab by pretending you're healthy. You rehab by admitting you're hurt—and letting the right Physician walk you through the process. For me, rebuilding faith wasn't about regaining religious momentum. It was about learning to walk again—slowly, humbly, dependently.

And surprisingly, that place of weakness became the strongest foundation I've ever stood on.

Rebuilding Starts with Presence, Not Promises

After everything collapsed, I wanted a reset button. A fresh start. A clean slate. A powerful comeback story that would erase the past and fast-forward to redemption.

Jesus offered something better.

Daily presence.

I wanted a detailed blueprint—steps, timelines, measurable progress. I wanted clarity I could execute and track. He offered a path. One step. One conversation. One honest prayer at a time.

Rebuilding faith after collapse doesn't look dramatic. It rarely feels heroic. It resembles learning to walk again after injury. Slow. Intentional. Often unimpressive. But deeply real.

There were no viral moments. No overnight transformation. Just steady presence. Quiet growth. Small choices that built momentum in the right direction.

And that's when I realized something powerful: God wasn't rebuilding my image. He was rebuilding my intimacy.

And intimacy grows through presence—not promises of instant change.

Why Shame Slows Spiritual Healing

Shame is loud when you fall. It pushes urgency. It demands speed. It whispers, "Fix this now. You should be further along. You've wasted too much time."

Shame demands performance. Grace restores trust.

For a long time, I carried the quiet belief that I needed to prove my repentance. That I had to compensate spiritually for the damage I'd caused. That if I just disciplined myself hard enough, I could accelerate healing.

But that's not relationship. That's self-punishment dressed up as spirituality.

Jesus never asked me to punish myself. He asked me to walk with Him. To sit. To listen. To stay.

Shame rushes. Grace rebuilds. And healing only moves at the pace of honesty.

When I stopped trying to fast-forward transformation—when I stopped measuring progress like a performance chart—I began to experience real change. Not flashy. Not immediate. But lasting.

Because transformation rooted in grace grows deep.

The Discipline Comes Back—But Different

Discipline is wired into me. As a coach, it shapes how I think, how I prepare, how I lead. And discipline absolutely has a place in faith.

But timing matters.

Discipline without healing becomes pressure. Discipline after surrender becomes purpose.

This time, discipline wasn't about:

- Making up for lost time
- Impressing God
- Outworking guilt
- Proving my seriousness

It became something different:

- Deep listening
- Honest aligning
- Staying intentionally close
- Practicing consistency rooted in love

Prayer wasn't a rigid routine—it became breath. Scripture wasn't ammunition for arguments—it became nourishment for my soul. Obedience wasn't pressure—it became trust.

Discipline returned—but not as punishment. As partnership.

Not as effort to earn God's approval—but as expression of love for a God who had already restored me.

And that difference is subtle—but powerful. Because when discipline flows from relationship, it energizes you instead of exhausting you. Rebuilding no longer feels like catching up. It feels like coming home.

Why the Right Church Matters After Collapse

This is where church became vitally important again.

Not a controlling church. Not a shame-based church. Not a performance-driven church. A genuinely healthy church.

After collapse, you are vulnerable. Your confidence is rebuilding. Your discernment is sharpening. And the environment you step into matters more than ever.

Today, I attend a life-giving church—one that strengthens relationship rather than replacing it. One that consistently points you toward Jesus instead of positioning itself as the exclusive gatekeeper to Him.

That distinction changed everything for me.

A truly healthy church:

- Walks alongside you—not over you
- Encourages healing—not hiding
- Welcomes honest questions—without instilling fear
- Produces freedom—not unhealthy dependence
- Reinforces Scripture—without manipulating emotion

A religious cult builds unwavering loyalty to its system. A healthy church fosters genuine intimacy with Christ. One tightens control when you're weak. The other strengthens you while you heal.

After collapse, spiritual discernment matters more than ever. You don't need pressure—you need presence. You don't need image management—you need truth spoken in love.

I didn't need to abandon church. I needed the right church.

And when you find a community that clears the path to Jesus instead of crowding it, rebuilding doesn't feel forced—it feels supported. It feels steady. It feels safe.

And in that kind of environment, healing doesn't just begin.

It deepens.

Rebuilding Faith Isn't Linear

Here's something no one tells you clearly enough: rebuilding faith is not a straight line.

Some days felt strong. Some days felt empty. Some days were filled with peace that surprised me. Other days felt painfully exposed—like every weakness was still under construction. There were moments of deep clarity, and there were moments of honest doubt. There were stretches where prayer flowed easily, and seasons where it felt quiet and slow.

But here's what never changed: relationship held.

Jesus didn't disappear when I struggled. He didn't withdraw when I felt inconsistent. He didn't shame me when I slowed down or needed to pause. He remained steady. Faithful. Present.

That's how trust rebuilds—not through bursts of intensity, but through quiet consistency.

In athletics, progress is rarely immediate. Some workouts feel explosive. Others feel frustrating. Some sessions leave you energized; others expose weakness. But if you stay committed, growth is happening beneath the surface. Muscles strengthen. Stamina builds. Coordination improves—even when you can't see it yet.

It's the same spiritually.

Not dramatic highs. Not emotional hype. But steady, daily presence. Small prayers. Honest conversations. Returning again and again.

That kind of consistency rebuilds confidence in a way intensity never can.

What Faith Looks Like After Collapse

Faith after collapse looks different.

Humbler.

Quieter.

Stronger in ways that aren't loud.

There's less talking—and more listening. Less image-crafting—and more integrity. There's less need to impress and more desire to align.

I stopped obsessing over the question, *"How do I look spiritually?"* And I started asking the only question that truly keeps me grounded:

"Am I staying honest and close?"

Honest with God. Honest with myself. Honest about where I'm strong—and where I'm not. Close in prayer. Close in Scripture. Close in conversations that matter.

That question protects me.

Because image can grow quickly. You can polish perception in a season. But intimacy grows slowly—and it lasts.

After collapse, faith becomes less about spotlight and more about substance. Less about proving and more about walking. Less about being seen and more about being formed.

And when you walk closely—even imperfectly—you discover something powerful: strength doesn't come from appearing solid. It comes from staying connected.

Connection holds you steady when circumstances shift. Connection steadies your leadership. Connection anchors your identity. And connection is what keeps everything else standing when pressure rises.

You're Not Behind—You're Being Rebuilt

If you've experienced collapse, read this slowly:

You're not disqualified.

You're not hopelessly delayed.

You're not broken beyond repair.

You're being rebuilt.

And rebuilt the right way.

High achievers hate setbacks. We measure everything against pace and progress. We compare seasons. We track timelines. When something falls apart, our instinct is to ask, *"How far behind am I now?"*

But rebuilding isn't falling behind. It's strengthening the foundation.

And stronger foundations always take longer.

In construction—and in faith—you don't rush footings. You dig deep. You clear debris. You reinforce what wasn't solid before. It's slower. Less visible. Often unimpressive from the outside. There's no applause for excavation work.

But it lasts.

And that's what Jesus is doing in seasons of collapse. He's not punishing you. He's fortifying you. He's not sidelining your calling. He's strengthening the character that will carry it.

Because what's rebuilt with Him won't crumble under pressure the way self-built systems do. The delay you feel may actually be development. And development always serves destiny.

You're not stuck. You're being strengthened at the root.

Reflection

What part of your faith needs compassionate rehabilitation instead of relentless pressure?

Is it your prayer life?

Your trust?

Your view of yourself?

Your understanding of grace?

Where are you demanding immediate performance when God may be inviting patient healing?

Rehabilitation isn't weakness. It's wisdom. And honest evaluation is the first step toward sustainable growth.

Heart Check

Right now—be honest:

Are you trying to rush healing?

Are you measuring progress with impatience?

Are you frustrated that transformation isn't moving faster?

Or are you learning to stay present with Jesus through the entire process?

Because presence matters more than pace.

Rushing healing often reopens wounds. Remaining present strengthens them. The goal isn't fast growth. It's real growth. And real growth carries durability that hype never can.

Simple Action Step

This week, stop asking God to fix everything instantly.

Don't demand overnight change.

Don't pressure yourself to leap ahead.

Instead, pray:

"Jesus, walk with me through this."

Not around it.

Not over it.

Through it.

Then pay attention.

Notice where peace settles. Notice where clarity grows. Notice the quiet strength forming underneath the surface. Notice how your reactions begin to soften. Notice how trust begins to stabilize.

Rebuilding with Jesus may not look dramatic. It may not be fast. It may not be flashy.

But it will be durable.

And durable faith is far more powerful than fast faith.

You're not behind.

You're being rebuilt.

And what God rebuilds—endures.

CHAPTER 7

What Healthy Leadership Looks Like After Failure

Failure changes how you lead—if you allow it to.

That shift isn't optional. It's necessary.

Before my collapse, leadership was something I did. It was output. It was visible results. It was intensity, vision-casting, driving outcomes, and carrying the room with force and energy. I measured leadership the same way I measured performance—by what could be seen, tracked, and celebrated.

After failure, leadership became something I was becoming.

And that difference is everything.

One path builds on image and performance. It looks strong. It sounds strong. It may even produce strong numbers—for a while. But eventually, it cracks under pressure because it was built on projection instead of depth.

The other path builds on integrity and trust. It grows slower. It's quieter. It doesn't always trend on a scoreboard. But it withstands storms because it's rooted deeper than applause.

In sports, failure exposes fundamentals. Film reveals what effort tried to hide. You can fake excellence for a few games—but the tape eventually tells the truth. It always does.

Life works the same way.

Failure stripped away my need to impress. It dismantled the leadership style I absorbed early on—lead loud, dominate space, hold tight control, never let them see weakness. That style can produce short-term results. It can intimidate. It can command. It can drive.

But long-term? It breaks people.

And eventually, it breaks the leader too.

Healthy leadership after failure begins with this realization: if you've never been broken, you can't truly protect others. Brokenness softens you. It deepens empathy. It increases discernment. It reshapes how you handle influence and responsibility.

Failure didn't disqualify me from leadership. It purified how I lead.

Authority That Has Been Humbled

Before failure, I confused authority with control.

I believed strong leadership meant a firm grip, decisive dominance, and clear hierarchy. If you were in charge, you set the tone. You tightened standards. You made sure everything stayed aligned—through pressure if necessary.

After failure, I learned something different: real authority flows from trust.

Healthy leadership never needs to intimidate people into submission. It doesn't manipulate situations to maintain control. It doesn't over-spiritualize decisions to avoid accountability. It doesn't demand unquestioning loyalty or silence honest concerns.

Those aren't strategies. They're symptoms of insecurity.

Authentic authority carries a quiet steadiness. It doesn't rush to prove itself. It doesn't posture for attention. It doesn't lean on titles or roles to validate identity. It leads from conviction—not ego.

That's how Jesus led.

He didn't intimidate. He didn't manipulate. He didn't elevate image over integrity. He led with love and truth held in powerful tension—clear standards, deep compassion.

Failure taught me this: leadership without humility is just amplified noise with a microphone.

Humility doesn't weaken authority. It purifies it.

And when authority is rooted in humility, people feel strengthened—not controlled. They feel trusted—not managed. They grow—not shrink.

Healthy Leaders Don't Replace God

One of the most dangerous dynamics I've observed—especially in faith environments—is when leaders subtly position themselves between people and God.

Sometimes it's intentional. Sometimes it's insecurity in disguise. Either way, the damage is real.

Healthy leadership always points away from itself.

A healthy leader says:

- ◆ "Go directly to Jesus—He's available."
- ◆ "Search Scripture—discover truth for yourself."
- ◆ "Learn to discern His voice."
- ◆ "Don't depend on me—develop your own walk."

Healthy leadership builds independence rooted in Christ.

Controlling leadership says:

- ◆ "You need my covering to stay protected."
- ◆ "Don't question my direction."
- ◆ "Trust me more than your own discernment."
- ◆ "Leaving equals disloyalty."

That's not shepherding. That's control.

Failure sharpened my discernment in this area dramatically. Once you've seen how easily influence can be misused—once you've felt the weight of your own blind spots—you become more careful with it.

Authentic leadership builds people who can thrive without you.

Unhealthy leadership builds people who fear life beyond you.

And that distinction matters deeply.

Because real leadership doesn't create followers who stay dependent. It develops leaders who walk confidently—with Jesus at the center, not a personality, platform, or program.

Once you've been humbled, you understand something powerful: you're not the source. You're a steward. And stewardship always protects what ultimately belongs to God.

Why Failure Makes You Safer as a Leader

After failure, I let go of the exhausting need to look like I had everything figured out.

That one decision changed how I lead more than any seminar, book, or strategy ever could.

People don't need flawless leaders. They need safe ones.

Safe leaders:

- Admit mistakes quickly and fully
- Acknowledge blind spots instead of defending them
- Invite honest feedback without retaliation
- Protect dignity—even in correction
- Refuse to weaponize Scripture or authority
- Value people more than systems or short-term results

Failure gave me empathy I simply couldn't manufacture before.

Before collapse, I could teach principles. After collapse, I understood pain. I knew what pressure does internally. I recognized the quiet voice of shame. I understood how easy it is to hide behind performance—and how difficult it is to admit struggle.

Because I had walked through personal collapse, I was no longer threatened by someone else's weakness. I wasn't intimidated by questions. I wasn't angered by struggle.

I was equipped to walk beside them in it.

And that's what makes leadership safe—not perfection, but empathy rooted in experience.

Broken leaders who heal properly don't become fragile.

They become steady.

They speak more carefully. They listen more deeply. They move with greater awareness. And that steadiness creates an atmosphere where others can grow without fear.

Healthy Leadership Creates Margin, Not Pressure

One of the clearest signs of unhealthy leadership is relentless pressure dressed up as passion.

Constant urgency.

Constant demands.

Constant guilt.

Constant push for "more."

It looks intense. It may even appear productive. But over time, it drains people. And then—worst of all—it blames them for being drained.

Healthy leadership is different.

It creates margin.

It encourages rest—not as weakness, but as wisdom. It honors seasons. It recognizes limits. It values sustainability over spectacle. It understands that long-term growth outlasts short-term hype.

Recovery isn't optional in sports. You can't train at maximum intensity every single day without injury. Muscle needs rest to rebuild stronger. The same principle applies spiritually and organizationally.

You cannot operate under nonstop emotional or spiritual pressure without consequences.

Jesus modeled this beautifully. He withdrew. He rested. He stepped away from crowds. He slowed His pace intentionally. He never confused frantic movement with faithful obedience.

Neither should we.

Healthy leaders understand something crucial: growth thrives in margin. Pressure may spark activity—but margin produces maturity.

And mature leaders protect that space fiercely. They guard their own rhythms. They refuse to drive people beyond sustainable pace. They recognize that healthy people build healthy cultures.

After failure, I stopped asking, "How much can we push?"

I started asking, "What pace preserves people?"

That shift transformed how I coach, how I lead, and how I measure success.

Because healthy leadership isn't about squeezing more out of people.

It's about building people strong enough to endure—and still love the journey.

The Church Matters—When Leadership Is Healthy

This is why I'm deeply grateful for my current church community.

Not because it's perfect. Not because it never makes mistakes. But because its leadership is healthy. And healthy leadership changes everything.

It's a church that strengthens each person's direct relationship with Jesus. It encourages authentic growth without manipulation. It welcomes real questions without fear. It produces freedom instead of dependence.

That difference is tangible. You can feel it.

I believe wholeheartedly in the Church. I believe it is essential. I believe community, worship, accountability, and shared mission are gifts from God. But those gifts only flourish when leadership is rooted in humility and truth.

A healthy church trains you to recognize God's voice—not replace it.

A healthy church equips you to walk confidently with Jesus— not cling anxiously to an institution.

A healthy church produces unmistakable fruit: peace, humility, love, clarity.

By contrast, a religious cult produces something very different. It produces fear. It tightens control. It demands blind loyalty to human authority. And that difference is not minor—it's critical.

Especially after failure.

When you've experienced collapse, you are more sensitive. You recognize tone more quickly. You can feel when leadership nurtures growth and when it quietly manipulates. Discernment sharpens in broken seasons. And that sharpened discernment doesn't just protect you—it protects the people you lead.

Because at the end of the day, leadership isn't about influence. It's about stewardship. And stewardship always points people upward—to Jesus—not inward to a personality.

Healthy leadership after failure doesn't look louder.

It looks steadier.

And steady leaders change lives in ways hype never can.

Leadership That Comes After Collapse Is Different

Leadership after collapse doesn't just adjust—it transforms.

There is a depth that only comes through being broken and rebuilt. Post-failure leadership carries a different tone. It speaks with more precision—and less noise. It listens with deeper attention and genuine curiosity. It moves at a steadier, more thoughtful pace. It protects vulnerable hearts fiercely. It values people far more than measurable outcomes.

There's less urgency to dominate every room. Less need to prove competence constantly. Less hunger for affirmation and applause.

It no longer feels necessary to win every debate, control every decision, or secure every spotlight.

Instead, leadership becomes centered on a far simpler question:

Am I being faithful in this moment?

Failure refines ego. It clarifies priorities. It exposes how fragile image-based leadership really is. You begin to understand that influence is not sustained by volume—but by consistency, humility, and trust.

Leadership after collapse isn't louder.

It's deeper.

It's anchored.

And that anchoring changes how you handle pressure, criticism, and responsibility. You no longer panic when questioned. You no longer overreact when challenged. You no longer equate disagreement with disloyalty.

You lead from identity—not insecurity.

And that shift reshapes every room you walk into.

What I Coach Differently Now

I coach differently today because I've been broken.

And I've been rebuilt.

I now lead the way I wish someone had led me earlier: with clarity instead of confusion. With honest truth instead of veiled threats. With real grace instead of relentless pressure. With clear expectations instead of manipulative shame. With accountability rooted in care—not ego.

I still value excellence. I still hold standards. I still believe discipline matters deeply.

But the tone is different.

The posture is different.

Before failure, correction sometimes carried edge. Now it carries intention. Before failure, accountability felt like tightening control. Now it feels like strengthening ownership. Before failure, weakness could feel inconvenient. Now it feels like sacred ground that must be handled carefully.

Leadership after failure isn't weaker.

It's stronger—because it's authentic.

There's no need to pretend. No need to posture. No need to protect image at the expense of people. When you've already been exposed and rebuilt, you're not afraid of transparency anymore.

And when leadership is authentic, people grow—not because they're afraid to fail, but because they're safe to learn.

That's the difference.

Authenticity produces longevity.

People stay. They develop. They trust. And trust is the soil where real growth happens.

Reflection

Have you experienced leadership that demanded rigid control instead of cultivating trust?

What did it feel like?

Did it build confidence—or create fear? Did it strengthen discernment—or silence questions? Did it develop you—or make you dependent?

Leadership always leaves a mark. Even when it's subtle. Even when it's well-intended.

The question is: what kind?

Take a moment to evaluate how those environments shaped you. Not with bitterness. Not with blame. But with clarity. Because clarity gives you choice. And choice gives you freedom to become a different kind of leader.

Heart Check

Do the leaders in your life consistently point you toward Jesus—

Or do they subtly position themselves as your primary source of safety and guidance?

Healthy leaders direct you upward.

Unhealthy leaders draw loyalty inward.

One cultivates freedom.

The other cultivates dependence.

Discernment here is essential. Because who you follow shapes who you become. And if your leaders are secure in Christ, they will not feel threatened by your growth. They will celebrate it.

Ask yourself honestly: does this leadership strengthen my relationship with Jesus—or simply my attachment to a system?

That answer will tell you more than any mission statement ever could.

Simple Action Step

This week, thank God intentionally for the leaders who helped you heal instead of merely perform.

Think about the ones who listened when you struggled. The ones who protected your dignity in correction. The ones who pointed you to Christ instead of positioning themselves as indispensable.

Express gratitude. Reach out if you can. Encourage them.

Then pray this simple, powerful prayer:

"Lord, make me that kind of leader.

Secure enough to release control.

Humble enough to admit fault.

Strong enough to protect the vulnerable.

Anchored enough to point people to You."

Because healthy leadership doesn't come from avoiding failure.

It comes from being rebuilt by the right hands.

And when you've been rebuilt with humility and truth, you don't just lead differently—

You lead safely.

And safe leaders don't just build teams.

They shape generations.

Chapter 8

Leading Yourself Before Leading Others

Every great coach I've ever respected understood this early—or learned it the hard way: you cannot lead others where you refuse to lead yourself. That isn't inspirational language. It's structural truth. In sports, it becomes obvious quickly. A coach who neglects his own preparation, conditioning, or discipline may command attention for a season, but eventually he loses the locker room. Players may comply, but they will not deeply follow. Credibility erodes quietly at first, then publicly. And once credibility erodes, influence fades—no matter how strong the personality.

Faith works the same way.

Before my collapse, I believed leadership was primarily about outward results. I measured everything by numbers—wins, growth, momentum, recognition. If the metrics were strong, I assumed I was leading well. But I neglected the most important responsibility I carried: my inner life. No one had truly taught me how to lead myself spiritually. Religion gave me routines. Athletics gave me discipline. Success gave me confidence. But none of those trained me to steward my heart.

And this is critical: an unled heart will eventually lead you somewhere you never intended to go.

You can manage systems. You can manage schedules. You can manage people. But if you do not lead yourself, your internal world will quietly begin steering your external one. And it rarely steers toward peace.

Discipline Without Direction Is Dangerous

Athletes understand discipline naturally. Structure. Repetition. Accountability. Early mornings. Hard conversations. Sacrifice. That part came easy to me. I didn't need convincing that discipline mattered—I lived inside it.

What did not come naturally was direction.

I trained my body relentlessly. I sharpened my mind intentionally. I developed my skills strategically. But I neglected my soul. Religion told me what to do. Sports trained me how to do it. But almost no one consistently asked the deeper question: Who are you becoming?

When pressure increased—success, money, influence, temptation—I realized something sobering. I had discipline. But I lacked alignment. Discipline without identity slowly morphs into self-reliance. And self-reliance eventually collapses under real pressure.

You can be disciplined and still deeply lost. You can be successful and still hollow. You can be respected and still dangerously unguarded internally.

True self-leadership demands more than effort. It demands alignment between what you do and who you are becoming. And alignment does not happen accidentally. It requires intentional reflection, intentional correction, and intentional surrender.

Self-Leadership Is About Awareness, Not Control

Before failure, I tried to control myself. After failure, I learned to lead myself. Those are not the same thing.

Control suppresses. Leadership observes. Control says, "Don't feel that. Don't show weakness. Don't admit struggle. Push through." Leadership asks better questions: "What's happening inside right now? Why am I reacting this way? What needs to be brought into the light?"

Healthy self-leadership begins with awareness—awareness of triggers, patterns, fatigue, loneliness, pride, fear, insecurity, emotional drift. Athletes watch film to correct mechanics. Leaders must "watch film" on their soul to sustain integrity.

If you do not examine what is happening internally, pressure will expose it externally. And exposure without preparation is painful.

The goal is not hyper-control. It is honest awareness. Awareness produces humility. Humility produces dependence. Dependence produces strength.

When you learn to lead yourself well—spiritually, emotionally, relationally—you stop leading others from ego. You lead from alignment. And aligned leaders do more than win seasons. They build legacies that last beyond their voice, their title, or their platform.

You Cannot Outsource Self-Leadership

One of the most subtle and dangerous lies in faith and leadership is this belief: "Someone else will cover me." A pastor. A mentor. A system. A title. Those relationships matter. Community is essential. Coaching sharpens you. But none of them can lead your inner life for you.

Church is vital. Accountability is necessary. Wise counsel is a gift. But nothing replaces daily, personal responsibility before God. That part is not negotiable.

Jesus did not say, "Follow your leader." He said, "Follow Me."

There is wisdom in leadership and value in spiritual guidance. But there is a line you cannot cross—you cannot outsource your intimacy with Christ. Self-leadership means owning your spiritual health, your boundaries, your rhythms, your honesty, your repentance, your rest.

No one else can pray in place of you. No one else can repent for you. No one else can cultivate your heart. They can guide you. They cannot replace you.

When leaders forget this, unhealthy dependence grows where maturity should. Real growth begins when you stop leaning on spiritual proximity—simply being around strong voices—and start cultivating spiritual responsibility.

Why Unled Leaders Hurt People

This is uncomfortable—but it's true. Unled people eventually lead from wounds instead of wisdom. Unled leaders create pressure instead of peace. Unled leaders demand what they themselves cannot give.

Before my collapse, I did not see it clearly—but I was leading from ego, insecurity, performance, and approval addiction. I never woke up intending to harm anyone. But intention does not override impact.

When you are not leading yourself well, you overreact to threats that aren't real. You avoid correction because it feels like attack. You tighten control when you feel insecure. You confuse loyalty with love.

Leadership amplifies whatever is inside you. If insecurity is inside you, insecurity multiplies. If pride is inside you, pride spreads. If fear is inside you, fear becomes culture.

Self-leadership is not optional if you want to lead others well. It is the foundation everything else rests on. You can have talent, charisma, and vision—but without self-leadership, all of it becomes unstable.

Leading yourself means staying aware of your motives. It means addressing your wounds instead of projecting them. It means confronting pride before it contaminates your team. It means choosing repentance before correction, reflection before reaction.

Because when you are internally led by Christ, you do not lead others from pressure. You lead from peace.

And peace—steady, anchored, unshaken peace—is far more powerful than control will ever be.

Leading Yourself Looks Unimpressive

This is where many high achievers quietly stumble.

Self-leadership rarely looks impressive. It doesn't trend. It doesn't collect applause. It doesn't draw followers. It won't earn you a standing ovation or a promotion. Most of the time, no one even knows you're doing it.

It's quiet.

It's slow.

It's unseen.

Self-leadership looks like saying no when saying yes would look stronger. It looks like resting when hustle feels more productive—and even more spiritual. It looks like admitting weakness before it costs you everything. It looks like staying honest when no one would ever know the difference. It looks like walking away from opportunities that shine brightly but don't align internally.

That doesn't look dramatic.

But it is foundational.

Athletes understand this at a deep level. Championships are built on boring consistency. No one cheers for correct footwork in practice. No one celebrates clean mechanics in a Tuesday drill. But you cannot win without mastering them. Sloppy fundamentals get exposed under pressure.

In the same way, you cannot lead others well if your integrity erodes when no one is watching.

God honors fundamentals. And leading yourself well is the fundamental most leaders quietly neglect.

Jesus Modeled Self-Leadership Perfectly

Before He led crowds, Jesus led Himself.

He withdrew from demands. He prioritized prayer. He embraced rest. He resisted temptation. He rejected shortcuts. He refused performance-driven validation. He did not confuse visibility with value.

Even Jesus—fully God, fully man—refused to lead outwardly without first leading inwardly.

That rhythm wasn't optional for Him. It was essential.

He didn't allow popularity to dictate His pace. He didn't let pressure override presence. He didn't build His identity on applause. His public authority flowed from private alignment.

If the Son of God required solitude, prayer, and internal clarity—how much more do we?

Self-leadership isn't weakness. It's wisdom.

And when you study how Jesus moved, you see something powerful: He never allowed external demand to outrun internal alignment. That principle still governs healthy leadership today.

What I Practice Now

After failure, I changed how I lead myself—radically.

I check my heart daily, not just my calendar. I protect quiet time as fiercely as training time. I refuse to ignore fatigue or emotional drift. I bring temptation into the light early, not after it festers. I no longer confuse busyness with obedience.

Self-leadership now means paying attention sooner.

Earlier conversations.

Earlier corrections.

Earlier repentance.

Because small misalignments ignored become major breakdowns exposed.

It's not about becoming flawless. It's about becoming honest. Radically, consistently honest. Not after crisis—but before it.

That discipline will never trend online. It won't grow your platform overnight. But it will protect your marriage. It will stabilize your calling. It will guard your integrity. It will preserve your legacy.

And that's worth more than applause.

Reflection

Where are you actively leading others while quietly neglecting yourself?

Be specific.

Is it your marriage?

Your rest?

Your prayer life?

Your emotional health?

Your integrity?

Where are you pouring outward while avoiding inward?

Honesty here isn't self-condemnation. It's leadership. Because the moment you become aware is the moment you begin to lead differently.

Heart Check

Are you managing your image—or stewarding your soul?

One builds reputation.

The other builds legacy.

Reputation impresses people.

Legacy impacts generations.

And the difference begins in private decisions no one sees.

Every unseen choice either strengthens your foundation—or slowly weakens it.

Simple Action Step

Today, ask Jesus one direct question:

"What am I ignoring inside myself right now?"

Don't defend.

Don't rationalize.

Don't immediately fix.

Just listen.

Because awareness always precedes healing.

Honesty always precedes growth.

And authentic leadership always begins inward—long before it is ever visible outward.

Lead yourself well in the quiet places.

That's where real strength is formed.

CHAPTER 9

BUILDING TEAMS WITHOUT BREAKING SOULS

One of the hardest—and most humbling—lessons I've learned as a coach and leader is this: you can win… and still lose people.

Early in my coaching career, I equated intensity with effectiveness. I believed pushing harder automatically produced better results. If effort increased, performance would increase. If pressure rose, standards would sharpen. That mindset made sense to me. It aligned with everything I had been trained to believe.

I measured success by output—wins, execution, stats, discipline, performance metrics. And in sports culture, that approach is often applauded. It gets attention. It builds reputation. It earns labels like "tough," "driven," and "demanding excellence."

But here's the truth many locker rooms never say out loud: pressure produces results. Presence sustains people.

I've seen teams look dominant on paper while relationally falling apart underneath. I've watched gifted athletes comply outwardly while quietly losing confidence inwardly. I've seen leaders rise in rank while their people slowly burned out beneath them.

At one point, I was part of that problem.

Not because I didn't care. But because I didn't understand.

I thought winning covered everything.

It doesn't.

Results impress.

Relationships endure.

And if you're serious about leading well, you have to build both.

When Winning Becomes the Only Metric

Sports culture rewards what can be measured—wins, stats, rankings, records, championships. Measurable success matters. Excellence matters. Accountability matters.

But leadership that only values metrics eventually devalues people.

When performance becomes the sole focus, subtle shifts begin to happen. Mistakes feel unsafe. Questions feel threatening. Weakness feels punishable. Relationships begin to feel conditional.

Athletes may execute—but they stop trusting.

Teams may function—but they don't flourish.

You get compliance—but not commitment.

Execution—but not connection.

And connection is what sustains teams long after the scoreboard resets.

Jesus never led with metrics alone. He cared about growth and excellence, but He valued people over performance. He corrected—but with compassion. He challenged—but always within relationship.

Great coaches understand this instinctively: winning matters—but never at the cost of breaking the very people you lead. Because broken confidence doesn't produce lasting greatness.

Secure people do.

And security is built through trust, not fear.

Breaking Souls Isn't Always Loud

When people imagine soul-breaking leadership, they think of yelling. Explosive anger. Public embarrassment. Harsh criticism.

Sometimes it looks like that.

But more often—it's quieter. More subtle.

It looks like constant pressure with no margin to breathe. It looks like high expectations paired with low empathy. It looks like relentless correction without meaningful encouragement. It looks like accountability without relationship. It looks like results celebrated loudly while people quietly go unseen.

No shouting required.

No malicious intent necessary.

Just unresolved pressure rolling downhill.

And here's what I've learned the hard way: unhealed leaders leak pressure. Unled leaders multiply it.

If you haven't processed your own insecurities, you project them. If you haven't confronted your own fear of failure, you transfer it. If you haven't learned how to rest, you create systems that exhaust everyone around you.

Soul-breaking leadership doesn't always announce itself.

It slowly drains joy.

It chips away at confidence.

It replaces trust with tension.

And the worst part? It can happen while everything still looks "successful."

Building strong teams isn't just about raising standards. It's about protecting souls while pursuing excellence. That balance—excellence with empathy—is where truly great leadership lives.

People Are Not Equipment

One of the subtle—and devastating—dangers in sports and leadership is this: we begin to objectify people.

Players become "assets."

Staff become "resources."

Volunteers become "roles."

People become pieces on a board.

Once that shift happens, culture quietly changes.

People don't burn out simply from hard work. Athletes are built for hard work. Leaders can handle intensity. What drains them is something deeper.

They burn out when they feel invisible.

They burn out when their value feels tied exclusively to performance.

When someone believes they are only as good as their last result, emotional disconnection begins. They may still show up physically. They may still execute the game plan. They may still smile in meetings. But internally, they pull back.

Not because they're weak.

Because they don't feel valued beyond output.

Jesus never treated people as tools for a mission. He never reduced them to roles. He didn't see fishermen as labor units or tax collectors as strategic assets. He saw sons. He saw daughters. He saw hearts.

Performance mattered—but people mattered more.

And if leadership ever reverses that order, something sacred begins to erode.

Teams don't thrive when they feel used.

They thrive when they feel known.

And being known is what gives people the courage to grow.

Presence Is the Currency of Healthy Teams

The strongest teams I've had the privilege of leading didn't simply train harder. They connected deeper. They knew each other beyond positions and stats. They understood tone, body language, silence. And that kind of awareness didn't happen by accident—it was built through presence.

Presence changes everything.

Presence means you notice when someone is quieter than usual. It means you sense emotional drift before it turns into disengagement. It invites honest conversations early—before small issues explode into locker-room fractures. Presence builds psychological safety long before conflict ever surfaces.

Healthy presence notices subtle shifts in attitude. It opens space for early conversations. It builds trust long before correction is needed. It strengthens culture before crisis ever hits.

When leaders are genuinely present, correction lands better. Accountability feels safe. Standards rise naturally. Loyalty grows authentically.

Why? Because presence creates trust. And trust turns feedback from something threatening into something transformational.

People don't need leaders who are impressive from a distance. They need leaders who are attentive up close.

You don't earn someone's best effort by being intimidating. You earn it by being engaged—by knowing their story, understanding their pressure, and caring about more than their performance line.

Presence isn't loud. It doesn't post about itself. It doesn't seek attention.

But it is powerful.

And over time, it compounds—building teams that don't just execute well, but trust deeply.

High Standards, Low Shame

This distinction matters deeply.

Grace does not lower standards. Presence does not remove accountability. Healthy leadership says clearly, "We expect excellence—and we genuinely care about you."

Both.

Not one or the other.

Jesus modeled this flawlessly. He challenged Peter. He corrected the disciples. He raised expectations. But He never crushed identity. He corrected behavior without humiliating the person. He called people higher without shaming them into hiding.

That's where so many leaders miss it.

Shame might spark temporary compliance. It might tighten behavior quickly. But it destroys confidence. It silences vulnerability. It teaches people to hide mistakes instead of learn from them.

Safety produces growth.

When someone knows they can fail without being labeled, they risk improvement. When someone knows they won't be publicly humiliated, they open up. If a person cannot fail safely, they cannot grow fully.

High standards with high shame create fear-based performance.

High standards with low shame create sustainable excellence.

And sustainable excellence is what builds championship cultures—on the field, in leadership, and in life.

Winning matters.

But protecting the soul of the people who win with you?

That matters even more.

What I Lead Differently Now

After my personal collapse—and the long rebuilding that followed—I changed how I build teams.

Not dramatically on the outside.

But deeply on the inside.

Now I prioritize honesty over image. I address issues early and calmly instead of explosively after pressure builds. I check in personally—not just professionally. I celebrate effort, growth, and integrity—not just outcomes. And I watch carefully for burnout long before it surfaces publicly.

Most importantly, I refuse to ask people to carry weight I'm unwilling to help shoulder.

That shift alone transformed everything.

True leadership isn't standing above the pressure with folded arms. It's standing with people under it. It's walking the practice field with them. It's sitting in difficult conversations without rushing to defend yourself. It's absorbing some of the stress so they don't drown in it alone.

Leadership used to feel like directing traffic.

Now it feels like building trust.

And trust always outlasts pressure.

Jesus Built Teams, Not Machines

Look at the disciples.

They were inconsistent. Emotionally reactive. Often confused. Quick to speak. Slow to understand. Prone to failure—sometimes spectacular failure.

By strict performance standards, they were unreliable.

But Jesus didn't replace them when they faltered. He stayed with them. He coached patiently. He corrected with love. He restored fully. He trusted deeply.

He didn't treat them like machines to maximize. He treated them like men to form.

And that formation changed everything.

They didn't transform the world because they were flawless. They transformed it because they were shaped relationally. They were strengthened through presence. They were refined through correction wrapped in love.

Jesus invested in process—not just productivity.

He built people who could stand because they had been strengthened in relationship.

Machines execute.

People grow.

And growth outlasts performance every time.

Reflection

Take this seriously:

Where might your leadership be producing performance—but quietly costing people?

Are results rising while morale is slipping? Are outcomes improving while confidence is eroding? Are you getting what you want—but losing who you lead in the process?

Be honest.

Because short-term performance that damages long-term health isn't leadership. It's pressure management.

And pressure management always collapses eventually.

Heart Check

After people interact with you—

Do they feel safer?

Or smaller?

Do they leave conversations more confident?

Or more cautious?

Do they feel trusted?

Or monitored?

That answer reveals more than any performance metric ever will.

Leadership leaves emotional residue.

Make sure yours leaves strength.

Simple Action Step

This week, affirm someone on your team for who they are—not just what they produce.

Call out integrity.

Notice character.

Recognize growth.

Not just stats.

Not just execution.

Not just outcomes.

Look them in the eye and say what you see beyond the scoreboard.

Then watch what happens.

Because connection builds endurance.

Presence protects souls.

And teams built on relationship don't just perform—

They last.

CHAPTER 10

WINNING THE QUIET BATTLE —
LEARNING TO PRAY IN PRIVATE

One of the most transformational moments of my life didn't happen in a church service. Not in a locker room. Not in some powerful comeback story that people could point to and celebrate. It happened in private—no microphone, no audience, no platform. Just me and God.

For most of my life, prayer had been something visible and structured. I knew when to bow my head. I knew the right words to use. I knew how to sound spiritual. But knowing how to pray and knowing how to talk to God are two very different things.

For years, my prayers were polished, safe, measured, and appropriate. But they weren't honest. And intimacy never grows in performance.

The turning point in my faith didn't come from learning more theology. It came when I finally learned how to sit quietly and simply speak—and then listen.

Prayer as Performance vs. Prayer as Relationship

As an athlete and coach, I understood preparation. You perform publicly the way you train privately. But spiritually, I had flipped that pattern. Public prayer felt natural. Private prayer felt uncomfortable. I could pray confidently in front of teams. I could pray before games. I could pray when it was expected.

But alone? There was silence. Distraction. Awkwardness.

Religion had given me routines, but it hadn't cultivated relationship. My prayers sounded rehearsed—careful, polite, and controlled. Not raw. Not vulnerable. Not desperate.

Eventually I realized something that changed everything: real transformation doesn't happen in rehearsed spaces. It happens in hidden ones. When no one is impressed. When no one is watching. When there's no applause for what you say. That's where relationship is either built—or exposed as hollow.

Private Prayer Is Where Leaders Are Formed

Every serious athlete knows games reveal character, but practice builds it. Faith works the same way. Private prayer is the weight room of the soul. It's where strength develops before pressure tests it. It's where alignment is formed before leadership requires it.

When I stopped performing and started speaking honestly, everything shifted. No scripts. No elevated language. No pretending I had clarity when I didn't. Just honesty.

"God, I don't know what I'm doing."

"God, I'm tired of being angry."

"God, I don't trust myself right now."

"God, if You don't lead me, I will drift."

Breakthrough didn't come through eloquence. It came through vulnerability.

And slowly, I began to sense His direction—not audibly, not dramatically—but clearly. Conviction felt steady. Peace felt real. Wisdom felt grounded.

Private prayer didn't make me flashy. It made me anchored. And anchored leaders don't panic under pressure. When you've wrestled privately, you lead publicly with steadiness. The quiet battle is where leadership is formed—not in front of crowds, but in front of God.

If you want to win where it matters most, you have to learn to pray when no one sees.

Waiting Is Part of Training

As athletes, waiting feels like losing. We want immediate results, quick fixes, clear answers, instant wins. Waiting feels passive, unproductive, even weak.

But here's what I learned: God doesn't rush formation. He trains timing as intentionally as He trains talent.

One of the hardest disciplines for me was learning to pray—and then wait. Not to rush the next decision. Not to force clarity. Not to manufacture movement just to feel productive. Waiting felt like weakness. It turned out to be wisdom.

Waiting sharpened my discernment. It exposed my ego. It revealed how quickly I try to take control when I don't like uncertainty. And it saved me from myself more times than I can count.

God's silence wasn't neglect. It was conditioning. Just like an offseason where the scoreboard isn't moving but strength is quietly being built underneath. Muscles develop through repetition. Endurance grows through steady tension.

Waiting builds internal strength you can't measure immediately. And when you finally move, you move grounded—not rushed.

Private Prayer Breaks Public Pressure

Private prayer began to change how I carried pressure. It gave me peace when answers were delayed. It clarified truth when emotions were loud. It slowed me down when ego wanted to move fast. It built confidence without arrogance and direction without anxiety.

The more I prayed privately and consistently, the less I reacted impulsively. I stopped chasing public validation because I was already secure in private connection.

That connection changed how I coached. I became calmer under pressure, more measured in conflict, less reactive to criticism. When your spirit is settled in private, public pressure loses its grip.

Private prayer steadies the internal storm before it spills into the locker room, the boardroom, or your home. And steadiness may be one of the most powerful leadership traits you will ever develop.

Jesus Modeled This First

Jesus didn't just pray publicly—He withdrew privately. Before major decisions. After exhausting days. Before choosing His team. Before facing the cross.

Solitude wasn't optional for Him. It was foundational. He never let public demands override private alignment.

If the Son of God needed quiet spaces to stay aligned, how much more do we? Especially leaders. Especially coaches. Especially high-capacity people carrying heavy responsibility.

The more influence you hold, the more you need alignment. The more people you lead, the more you need solitude.

Waiting, praying, withdrawing—those aren't signs of weakness. They are disciplines of strength. When you begin to see waiting as training rather than delay, you start to trust that what God is building in you during quiet seasons will sustain you when the spotlight returns.

Real leadership isn't formed in noise. It's formed in stillness. And stillness is where strength is conditioned.

What I Practice Now

My private prayer life isn't necessarily long.

But it is consistent. Fiercely consistent.

Some days it's quiet. Some days it's emotional. Some days it's just one honest sentence whispered before the day begins. But it's always real. There's no script anymore. No polished tone. No performance. Just presence.

I've learned that depth isn't measured in minutes. It's measured in sincerity. Ten honest minutes can shape a day more than an hour of distracted words. What God seems to desire most isn't eloquence—it's accessibility. A heart that shows up. A mind that slows down. A leader who admits he needs guidance before he gives it.

Over time, I've discovered a few deeply freeing truths: I don't have to impress God with eloquence. I don't have to rush Him for answers. I don't have to carry tomorrow's burdens today. And I don't have to lead without listening first.

That last one changed everything.

Leadership gets loud. Demands increase. Expectations stack up. Voices compete for your attention. Pressure tries to define you before you've even taken a breath. Private prayer anchors me before all of that starts pulling. It grounds me before external noise tries to shape internal identity. It reminds me that I am led before I ever attempt to lead.

And when you are consistently grounded in private, you don't get shaken as easily in public.

Reflection

Be honest with yourself:

Have you been praying to be heard by others—or praying to be known by God?

Have your words been shaped for impact—or for intimacy?

Prayer isn't a performance review. It's a relationship. And relationships deepen when we drop the script and bring the truth.

Heart Check

Is there space in your life that belongs only to you and God?

No agenda. No preparation. No expectation to sound spiritual. No audience. Just honesty.

If every spiritual moment in your life is public, you may be building image instead of intimacy. Private space protects alignment. It softens ego. It allows clarity to form quietly before the day becomes chaotic.

Without that sacred space, pressure eventually fills the gap.

Simple Action Step

This week, set aside ten quiet minutes. No phone. No checklist. No agenda.

Don't ask for answers. Don't rehearse phrases. Just say, "God, I'm here." And then wait. Not impatiently. Expectantly.

Let the silence stretch. Let your mind settle. Let honesty rise.

That's where wisdom begins. That's where leaders are rebuilt from the inside out. That's where the unseen work—the kind that no one applauds but everyone eventually benefits from—takes place in your soul.

Commit to that quiet consistency, and you'll discover something powerful: strength doesn't start with noise. It starts with presence.

CHAPTER 11

HEARING GOD WITHOUT FORCING DIRECTION

As an athlete and a coach, I was trained to decide quickly. See the field. Read the situation. Make the call. Trust your instincts. In competition, hesitation gets you beat. That mindset served me well in sports, where decisive action builds confidence and momentum. But when I began rebuilding my faith, I unknowingly carried that same urgency into my relationship with God—and it nearly undermined everything He was trying to shape in me.

When I started praying more intentionally, I didn't just want guidance—I wanted direction on demand. Tell me where to go. Tell me what to do. Confirm the plan. Lay out the timeline. And if God didn't answer quickly enough, I would begin filling in the silence myself. I would interpret delay as opportunity or assume that movement meant approval. Looking back, I see the tension clearly. I wasn't listening. I was forcing. I wasn't seeking alignment; I was seeking confirmation. That kind of pressure might win a game, but it will distort a relationship. Faith doesn't flourish under frantic urgency. It grows through patient attentiveness.

Over time, I realized that I had been trying to move God at the speed of my ambition rather than learning to move at the pace of His wisdom. That realization humbled me. It forced me to confront how deeply I equated momentum with maturity. But spiritual growth doesn't accelerate because you demand it. It deepens because you surrender to it.

Why High-Capacity Leaders Struggle to Hear God

High achievers rarely struggle with effort. We struggle with control. We are wired to fix problems quickly, take full responsibility, push relentlessly forward, and create unstoppable momentum. That wiring helps us compete at high levels. It sharpens instincts and strengthens resolve. But spiritually, that same wiring can create internal noise.

When many leaders pray, we often pray with an outcome already outlined. "God, bless what I'm about to do." "God, confirm the decision I've already made." "God, open the door I'm pushing on." We may not realize it, but sometimes we are asking for validation more than direction. Relationship with Jesus is not a strategic playbook you execute flawlessly; it is a walk you remain attentive to daily. Walks require pace. Walks require awareness. Walks require listening. You cannot sprint your way through intimacy.

For me, learning to hear God meant loosening my grip on outcomes. It meant acknowledging that my strength in execution could become weakness in surrender. It required me to step back and ask not, "How do I make this happen?" but rather, "What is God shaping in me here?" That subtle shift changed how I prayed, how I waited, and how I led. Leaders who are capable of generating momentum must also learn to cultivate stillness. Without stillness, we risk confusing activity with alignment.

God Speaks Best When You Stop Forcing Outcomes

One of the most powerful lessons God taught me was simple but transformative: clarity does not come from pressure; it comes from posture. For years, I believed that if I prayed harder, longer, louder, or more strategically, God would respond faster. What I was really doing was trying to manage the timeline. I was attempting to accelerate answers through intensity. But God does not shout over frantic souls. He speaks into surrendered ones.

When I finally stopped demanding answers and began practicing presence, everything shifted. I stopped viewing silence as rejection and started recognizing it as formation. I began to notice His voice—not as loud instructions from heaven, but as wisdom settling steadily in my spirit. Sometimes it felt like peace that quieted anxiety when decisions loomed. Sometimes it felt like conviction that pierced through confusion. Other times it was a gentle nudge to wait, a restraint that protected me from rushing ahead, or a redirection that made little sense in the moment but revealed perfect timing later.

That kind of clarity cannot be forced. It is cultivated. It grows in a heart willing to pause and listen. As leaders, we often equate strength with decisiveness. Yet I have learned that spiritual strength is often revealed in restraint. When you stop forcing outcomes, you create space for God to form wisdom. And wisdom leads with far greater precision than pressure ever could.

Hearing God is less about extracting instructions and more about developing intimacy. It is about walking closely enough with Him that you recognize His rhythm. And for those of us trained to act fast, learning to slow down may be the most courageous leadership decision we ever make.

The Difference Between Impulse and Discernment

As a coach, I had to learn the critical difference between a reaction and a read. A reaction is emotional and immediate. A read is informed and intentional. In competition, the athletes who last are the ones who learn to slow the moment down internally, even when everything around them is moving fast. That same distinction applies spiritually in a powerful way.

Impulse is loud. It rushes. It demands movement. It thrives on adrenaline and urgency. Discernment, on the other hand, is steady. It reveals rather than pressures. Impulse says, "Do something now!" Discernment gently asks, "Is this truly Mine to carry?" Impulse feels productive. Discernment feels patient. Impulse wants to relieve anxiety quickly. Discernment seeks alignment first.

When I began slowing down long enough to discern rather than react, I made a humbling discovery: I had often confused urgency with obedience. Just because something felt pressing didn't mean it was God's assignment. Just because an opportunity appeared didn't mean it required immediate action. I realized that God was not silent—I was simply too loud on the inside. My ambition, fear, and desire to move forward were drowning out the subtle clarity He was offering. Learning to quiet that internal noise became one of the most transformative disciplines of my leadership journey.

Waiting Is Not Passive—It's Trained Trust

Waiting used to feel like weakness to me. In sports, waiting costs you reps. In leadership, waiting can feel like falling behind while others move ahead. Everything in my training had conditioned me to equate movement with progress. But in relationship with Jesus, waiting is not inactivity. It is trained trust.

Waiting boldly declares, "I don't need to rush this." It says, "I trust You to lead at the right time." It admits, "I don't need full clarity today in order to remain faithful today." That kind of waiting is not passive; it is deeply active. It is the deliberate decision to rest your hands when you want to take control.

Waiting trains humility. It breaks the grip of ego. It exposes whether your driving force is fear or faith. Are you moving because you trust God—or because you're anxious about losing momentum? These are not easy questions for high-capacity leaders to face. Yet every single time I chose to wait instead of forcing a decision, God proved faithful in ways I could not have orchestrated. The outcome didn't always come on my preferred timeline. But it always aligned perfectly with His. Waiting reshaped my pace, my confidence, and my understanding of what true strength looks like.

God Often Speaks Through Restraint

Some of the clearest guidance I have ever received did not come in the form of a green light. It came as a firm no. It came as a protective "not yet." It came as a door that remained stubbornly closed no matter how hard I pushed. At first, that frustrated me. I questioned it. I wrestled with it. I wondered if I had misunderstood. But over time, those closed doors became some of the greatest gifts God ever gave me.

God's restraint protected me from returning to destructive patterns that once controlled my life. It shielded me from leading out of selfish ambition instead of divine alignment. It guarded me from saying yes to good opportunities that would have quietly derailed God's best plans. What once felt like denial revealed itself as protection.

Silence is not absence. Delay is not rejection. Restraint is often mercy in disguise. When God says no, He is not withholding your future. He is refining it. And when He says wait, He is not limiting your impact. He is strengthening your foundation. Learning to recognize restraint as guidance rather than punishment transformed how I respond to closed doors. Instead of forcing them open, I now step back and ask what God may be building behind the scenes.

Discernment grows in that posture. Trust deepens there. And leaders who learn to embrace restraint often walk into doors they never could have forced on their own.

What Hearing God Looks Like Now

Hearing God today looks far less dramatic than I once imagined—and far more steady, reliable, and life-giving. Early in my faith journey, I expected clarity to arrive with bold certainty or unmistakable signs. I assumed direction would feel urgent, loud, or obvious. But over time, I have come to recognize that God's guidance is often quiet, consistent, and deeply settling.

Now, hearing God often manifests as an unshakable peace that refuses to leave even when circumstances feel uncertain. At other times, it appears as a persistent unease that gently cautions me to pause. Sometimes it is a particular passage of Scripture surfacing repeatedly in different settings, as though God is underlining it in my life. Other times it is wise counsel from trusted voices that confirms what He has already been whispering in my spirit. And occasionally, it is a closed door that redirects my path without condemnation or confusion.

I no longer need a voice booming from heaven to feel secure. What I need is alignment. Alignment in my spirit. Alignment between conviction and action. Alignment between timing and trust. That alignment consistently forms when I release control and resist the urge to force the next step. Clarity does not require spectacle; it requires surrender. And the more willing I am to yield, the more consistently I recognize His leading.

Reflection

Take a moment and consider this honestly: where in your life are you pushing hard for direction instead of practicing patient discernment? Is there a decision you are trying to finalize prematurely? An opportunity you are trying to create instead of waiting to see if it unfolds naturally? Sometimes our frustration with silence reveals more about our fear of waiting than about God's willingness to speak. Discernment grows in stillness, not in pressure.

Heart Check

Ask yourself with sincerity: are you listening to truly hear God—or are you listening for permission to pursue what you already desire? There is a meaningful difference. One posture seeks alignment. The other seeks validation. One is rooted in humility. The other is shaped by urgency. Hearing God requires an open heart, not a predetermined conclusion.

Simple Action Step

This week, when you feel pressure mounting to make a decision, pause and pray a different kind of prayer. Instead of asking for speed or confirmation, pray:

"Jesus, I trust You completely to lead. If You want me to move, make it unmistakably clear. If You want me to wait, fill me with Your perfect peace."

Then resist the instinct to force momentum. Stay present. Pay attention to what settles and what stirs. Notice whether peace strengthens or pressure increases. God consistently speaks to those who are willing to follow—not to those attempting to control the route. As you practice this posture, you will discover that discernment becomes clearer, trust becomes steadier, and leadership becomes more anchored in wisdom than urgency.

CHAPTER 12

LEADING FROM PEACE INSTEAD OF PRESSURE

For much of my life, pressure felt like fuel. As an athlete and later as a coach, pressure was normal—expected, even necessary. It sharpened focus, created urgency, and separated contenders from pretenders. If you couldn't handle pressure, you didn't survive in competitive environments. You learned quickly to embrace it, even wear it like armor.

So when I stepped into leadership—coaching teams, building programs, mentoring athletes, and running organizations—I carried that same mindset with me. Push harder. Move faster. Demand more. Absorb everything yourself. I believed pressure was proof that I cared deeply and led seriously. I told myself that intensity equaled impact.

But over time, I began to see the cracks. Pressure did not build strength the way I thought it would. It created tension in my spirit and distance in my relationships. It wore down my joy. It strained the very people I wanted to help grow. What I once viewed as leadership was actually unsustainable urgency. It was quietly draining my soul and eroding the health of the culture around me. The realization was humbling: pressure alone is not leadership. In excess, it is corrosion.

Pressure Can Get Results—but It Can't Produce Wholeness

There is no denying that pressure can generate results—at least for a season. You can squeeze performance from people. You can motivate through fear or urgency. You can achieve compliance, hustle, and even impressive wins. Short bursts of intensity may look productive on the surface.

But pressure cannot sustain people. It cannot cultivate deep peace or lasting health. Over time, pressure produces predictable outcomes:

- Burnout that drains creativity and joy
- Resentment that slowly poisons relationships
- Hidden struggles masked by outward performance
- Broken trust that weakens team culture
- Surface wins that carry hidden emotional costs

I saw this pattern in sports. I experienced it personally in leadership. And for years, I justified it with familiar phrases: "We're grinding." "This is what it takes." "No excuses." Those words sounded strong, but they concealed the toll being taken.

The truth I eventually had to face was simple and transformative: Jesus never led from pressure. Not once. He did not manipulate urgency to prove commitment. He did not confuse stress with strength. He pursued excellence without sacrificing wholeness. That distinction reshaped how I evaluate leadership today.

Jesus Led From Peace, Not Panic

One of the most uncomfortable yet freeing realizations I encountered was this: Jesus was never rushed, and He was never anxious. Crowds pressed in around Him. Needs were constant. Urgent demands followed Him everywhere. Yet He did not allow urgency to dictate His pace.

He withdrew when needed. He rested intentionally. He prayed consistently. He waited for timing to unfold. He moved with purpose, not panic. The mission He carried was urgent beyond comprehension, yet His demeanor remained anchored in peace.

This confronted my assumptions about leadership. I had been attempting to lead for God while ignoring how Jesus actually led with God. I had equated tension with effectiveness and stress with dedication. Yet the example before me was radically different. Peace did not mean passivity; it meant alignment. Peace meant anchored confidence that allowed Him to move deliberately, not reactively.

Leading from peace does not eliminate urgency. It transforms how you respond to it. Peace anchors you when demands rise. Peace steadies your voice when others panic. Peace preserves clarity when circumstances grow loud.

Learning to lead from peace instead of pressure has been one of the most refining shifts of my journey. It required me to slow down, to trust more deeply, and to recognize that urgency is a condition of the environment—not a condition of my spirit. When peace leads, pressure loses its power to control. And leaders who operate from peace do not merely achieve results—they build cultures that endure.

Pressure Is Often a Sign of Control, Not Calling

One of the hardest truths I ever had to face was this: much of the pressure I carried was not born out of commitment to excellence. It was born out of fear. Fear of failure. Fear of disappointing others. Fear of losing momentum. Fear of not being enough. I told myself that the constant internal drive was proof of dedication, but when I slowed down long enough to examine it honestly, I realized it was often insecurity wearing the mask of leadership.

Pressure whispers, "If I don't push this, it will fall apart." It convinces you that everything depends on your intensity. Peace, however, speaks differently. Peace says, "If God is in this, He can carry what I cannot." Pressure tightens your grip on outcomes, people, and timelines. Peace loosens that grip and reminds you that leadership is stewardship, not ownership. True, transformative leadership requires open hands, not clenched fists. When your hands are open, you can hold responsibility without being crushed by it. When they are clenched, even small challenges feel threatening.

The more I surrendered control, the more I recognized that calling never demands panic. Calling invites trust. Fear fuels pressure. Faith fuels peace. That distinction reshaped not just how I led, but how I lived.

Peace Changes the Atmosphere of Leadership

When I began leading from peace instead of pressure, the shift was not dramatic in the beginning, but it was unmistakable over time. Conversations became more honest. Decisions were made more thoughtfully. The pace slowed just enough to allow clarity to rise. People began to feel safer telling the truth—even when the truth involved mistakes.

Peace does not weaken leadership. It anchors it. Anchored leadership has roots deep enough to withstand storms without spreading anxiety to everyone else. When peace governs your spirit, you are able to respond rather than react. You correct without humiliating. You uphold high standards without creating hostility. You lead with conviction, not control.

Peace empowers leaders to:

- Respond thoughtfully instead of reacting impulsively
- Correct with compassion without crushing confidence
- Maintain strong standards without stirring fear
- Provide clarity without suffocating autonomy

People need direction, but they need safety even more. They need to know that mistakes will be addressed with wisdom, not volatility. That culture begins with a leader who has learned to settle their own heart first. Peace radiates outward. It shapes tone, timing, and trust. And over time, it changes the entire atmosphere of leadership.

You Can't Give Peace You Don't Possess

Perhaps the most humbling realization in my journey was this: I could not lead others into peace while I was internally operating from pressure. No amount of motivational talk could cover the tension people sensed in me. Leadership always transfers what lives inside it. If I was anxious, anxiety leaked. If I was restless, restlessness spread.

That realization required changes. Real changes. I had to slow my pace to something sustainable. I had to guard my prayer life as a non-negotiable priority. I had to detach my identity from outcomes and performance metrics. I had to stop stepping in to rescue situations God had not assigned to me.

Leading from peace begins privately before it ever shows up publicly. It forms in how you sit with God in silence, how you respond when stress mounts, how you define success when results fluctuate, and how you navigate seasons of uncertainty. Peace is not a posture you manufacture for others. It is a gift you receive in surrender.

When peace lives inside you, it steadies your leadership. It allows you to move confidently without moving frantically. It keeps your voice measured when others are overwhelmed. And it reminds you that true authority flows not from intensity, but from alignment. Leaders who operate from peace do more than achieve results—they cultivate environments where people can grow without fear.

Pressure Motivates Fear. Peace Builds Trust.

Pressure-driven leadership constantly asks a question that lingers beneath the surface: *Are you keeping up?* It measures pace, productivity, and output with a restless edge. Even when intentions are good, pressure often creates an environment where people feel evaluated more than valued. The underlying tone becomes urgency instead of unity.

Peace-driven leadership asks something very different: *Are you okay—and are we aligned?* It still cares about progress and excellence, but it refuses to sacrifice people at the altar of performance. Peace does not remove standards; it simply roots them in stability rather than anxiety.

Pressure can produce short-term wins. It can spark momentum and create bursts of productivity. But over time, pressure wears people down. It chips away at creativity, erodes morale, and drains resilience. Peace, on the other hand, builds trust. It establishes long-term health. And healthy teams do not merely endure—they flourish. They accomplish meaningful work with greater depth, greater collaboration, and greater impact.

I have learned that intensity may impress temporarily, but peace sustains powerfully. Trust grows in steady environments. Loyalty strengthens when people feel secure. And the most effective teams I have ever led were not the most pressured—they were the most grounded.

What Leading From Peace Looks Like Now

Leading from peace today looks intentional and disciplined in a different way. It means refusing to rush critical decisions simply because anxiety is loud or outside expectations are pressing. It means inviting God into moments of tension before crafting a response. It means allowing silence to linger rather than filling it with hurried explanations or controlling language.

Leading from peace also requires trust—trust that obedience matters far more than optics, and that long-term alignment outweighs short-term applause. I have learned to remember that results ultimately belong to God. My role is faithfulness. When I shift responsibility from controlling outcomes to stewarding obedience, something profound changes internally.

I still care deeply. I still lead decisively. I still pursue excellence with passion and discipline. But I no longer sacrifice peace to prove that I am serious. I no longer equate tension with commitment. I have discovered that peace itself is evidence of healthy leadership. It signals trust. It reflects alignment. It strengthens culture. Peace does not weaken resolve; it clarifies it.

Reflection

Consider honestly where in your leadership you may be operating from pressure rather than peace. Are you moving quickly because clarity is present—or because anxiety is loud? What would change tomorrow if you led from calm confidence instead of urgent control? Take time to evaluate the tone you set, the pace you maintain, and the posture you embody.

Heart Check

Ask yourself a straightforward question: do the people you lead experience you as calm and anchored—or tense and driven? Do they feel steadied by your presence, or stretched by your pressure? Leadership culture is shaped by the internal condition of the leader. If you prioritize peace, your environment will begin to reflect it.

Simple Action Step

This week, before making any difficult leadership decision, pause intentionally and pray:

"Jesus, am I responding from peace—or from pressure? If this is from You, settle my spirit. If this is from fear, slow my step."

Then act from what settles, not from what shouts. Strong leadership is not measured by volume or urgency. It is revealed in steadiness. The strongest leaders are not the loudest or the most intense—they are the ones grounded deeply enough to lead others without losing themselves in the process.

CHAPTER 13

LEARNING TO TRUST GOD'S PACE OVER YOUR OWN

One of the most difficult adjustments I've had to make—as an athlete, a coach, and a leader—is accepting that God's pace is rarely my pace. That realization has reshaped not only my faith, but the way I lead, decide, and measure progress. I was raised in competitive environments where speed was not merely encouraged; it was celebrated. Fast decisions. Fast growth. Fast wins. Momentum was everything. If you hesitated, you lost your edge. If you slowed down, you risked being passed.

So when I began walking more intentionally with Jesus, I carried that same urgency into my prayer life. I wanted answers quickly. Clarity immediately. Direction now. I prayed like a coach sketching out a final play with seconds left on the clock, expecting God to respond on my timeline and match my intensity with immediate movement. Yet He did not. And at first, that silence felt confusing—even frustrating. Over time, I began to understand that what I interpreted as delay was actually formation. God was not ignoring my urgency; He was reshaping it.

The deeper lesson was this: faith is not about accelerating outcomes. It is about aligning your heart with God's rhythm. That shift required patience I had not yet cultivated. But patience became the training ground where trust matured.

God Is Never Late—But He's Rarely Early

Timing often becomes the greatest tension point in our relationship with God. We may know what we feel called to do. We may sense readiness and even hunger for the next season. But His movement can feel slow, quiet, or delayed in ways that stretch our comfort.

Through experience—sometimes painful, always transformative—I've learned that delay is not denial. It is divine preparation. Silence is not absence. It is sacred space where growth deepens. Waiting is not wasted time. It is where character is refined. God works at a pace that forms us completely rather than merely advancing plans efficiently.

His timeline serves a purpose greater than productivity. While I often measured time by output, God measured it by alignment. I wanted speed because speed felt like success. God prioritized depth because depth sustains success. Every delay I once questioned eventually revealed layers of preparation I did not see at the time. Patience became less about endurance and more about trust—trust that He sees the full picture while I only see the next step.

Why High-Capacity People Struggle With God's Timing

High-capacity leaders often struggle most with waiting because we equate movement with progress. In athletics, more repetitions typically lead to improvement. More effort often produces better results. That formula works in many arenas of life. But spiritual formation does not always follow the same rhythm.

God frequently slows us down to build something within us before releasing something through us. That deceleration is not punishment; it is protection and preparation. I wanted assignment—God wanted alignment. I wanted clarity—God wanted trust. I wanted to run forward—God wanted me to walk with Him first.

That distinction was humbling. It exposed how often my ambition outpaced my maturity. Yet as I began to yield to His timing, I saw that growth was occurring in the quiet seasons. Trust strengthened. Character deepened. Dependence matured. When movement finally came, it carried stability rather than strain.

Learning to trust God's pace means recognizing that formation precedes expansion. It requires believing that delay can be development. And for leaders accustomed to speed, it may be one of the most transformative disciplines we ever embrace.

Pace Reveals Who You Trust

One of the most uncomfortable but transformative truths I have learned is this: when I rush, I am often trusting my urgency more than God's wisdom. Pace exposes belief. It reveals what I truly think about control, timing, and responsibility.

When I move too quickly, I have to ask myself hard questions. Do I genuinely believe God is in control, or do I subconsciously believe everything depends on my pressure? Do I trust Him with outcomes—or only with good intentions? Am I moving because He is leading, or because I feel anxious about losing momentum?

Fast faith can feel productive. It feels decisive. It gives the illusion of progress. Slow faith, however, feels vulnerable. It requires surrender. It demands that I release control over timing and appearances. Yet it is precisely in that vulnerability that real trust is formed. When I slow down intentionally, I create room to hear more clearly, align more deeply, and act more wisely. Pace is not just about speed; it is about trust in action. And my rhythm often reveals whether I am rooted in faith or driven by fear.

God Trains in Seasons, Not Sprints

Athletes understand the importance of seasons. There is off-season preparation where foundations are strengthened. There is in-season execution where effort becomes visible. There is recovery, where muscles repair and endurance grows. There is re-evaluation, where strategy is refined. No athlete expects peak intensity to remain constant all year without consequence.

Yet spiritually, many of us demand permanent in-season intensity. We expect constant forward movement, visible results, and uninterrupted clarity. But God does not train that way. He works in seasons. He allows waiting seasons that cultivate patience. He ordains hidden seasons that secure identity. He creates quiet seasons that deepen roots and reset seasons that clarify vision.

These seasons are not evidence of inactivity; they are evidence of intention. God is not hurried by our timelines. He is committed to sustainability. Just as an athlete cannot perform at peak capacity without preparation and recovery, leaders cannot sustain impact without formative seasons. Recognizing the value of each season reshapes how we interpret delay. What appears slow may actually be strategic. What feels hidden may be foundational.

Waiting Develops Muscles You Cannot Grow Any Other Way

Waiting is not passive—it is developmental. It strengthens qualities that cannot be cultivated through speed. Waiting builds patience that sustains through adversity. It develops discernment that sees beyond surface-level excitement. It forms humility that attracts divine grace. It nurtures dependence that invites supernatural strength. And it matures emotional steadiness that stabilizes leadership under pressure.

There are no shortcuts to these qualities. I have learned that God often delays direction until my heart is steady enough to carry the weight. He refines motives until they are clean enough to steward opportunity wisely. He secures identity until it is strong enough to withstand scrutiny and success. He slows my pace until it is surrendered enough to follow rather than rush ahead.

Rushed leaders may experience early success, but sustainability is another matter. Impact that endures requires formation. Waiting shapes that formation. It forges internal strength that external achievement alone cannot provide. Trusting God's pace means believing that what He builds slowly will stand firmly. And in leadership, endurance often matters far more than initial speed.

Peace Is the Indicator You're in Step

Over time, I have adopted a simple but powerful filter in my life: peace reveals alignment. When I am walking at God's pace, there is a steady peace present—even when I do not yet have full clarity. When I begin running ahead of Him, anxiety creeps in—even if the decision appears sound and the plan looks impressive on paper.

Peace does not mean the absence of difficulty. It does not guarantee that circumstances will be easy or comfortable. What peace signals is alignment. It is the quiet confidence that comes from knowing you are moving in step rather than sprinting ahead. God's pace may feel slower than my preference, but it carries rest. My pace, when driven by urgency, may appear productive, but it often carries internal pressure that drains the soul.

I have learned that peace is not optional for sustainable leadership. It serves as an internal indicator that my heart is positioned correctly. When peace is present, I can move forward with steadiness. When anxiety dominates, it is often an invitation to pause, reassess, and realign. Recognizing this distinction has protected me from unnecessary strain and redirected me toward healthier rhythms.

Learning to Wait Without Drifting

Waiting with God is not passive resignation. It is active, intentional trust. It is not disengagement; it is disciplined patience. Waiting well looks like praying sincerely without attempting to manufacture answers. It looks like working faithfully without striving to control outcomes. It means continuing to show up consistently without demanding immediate results.

Waiting also requires attentive listening—speaking less and observing more. It means obeying the next step clearly revealed without insisting on a complete blueprint for the future. Faith does not mature only when everything makes sense. It grows when you continue walking even while certain questions remain unanswered.

Drifting happens when waiting turns into apathy. Trust, however, remains engaged. It stays connected, responsive, and obedient. When I learned to wait with intention rather than frustration, I discovered that waiting seasons often carry some of the most formative growth. They deepen character, refine motives, and build endurance. Leaders who wait well develop resilience. They learn that patience is not weakness but preparation.

Reflection

Consider honestly where you might be attempting to force momentum instead of trusting God's timing. Is there an area of your leadership or personal life where urgency feels self-imposed rather than Spirit-led? What might shift if you slowed down long enough to evaluate whether your pace reflects alignment or anxiety?

Heart Check

Examine the state of your heart. Do you sense peace in the season of waiting, or does frustration dominate your decisions? Are you moving because you trust God's timing, or because you fear missing opportunity? What would it truly look like to surrender your personal timeline and entrust it entirely to Him?

Simple Action Step

Identify one specific area where you have been rushing the process. Name it honestly. Then surrender it intentionally. Each day this week, pray:

"Jesus, help me slow to Your perfect pace, even when I do not understand it. Teach me to trust what You are forming in me, not just what You are producing through me."

God's pace may challenge your patience and confront your desire for control. Yet it will strengthen your leadership, deepen your faith, and restore your spirit in ways rushing never could. Nothing formed at His pace is wasted. Every season carries purpose. And leaders who learn to move in step rather than sprint ahead discover a steadiness that outlasts any moment of temporary momentum.

CHAPTER 14

UNDERSTANDING YOUR CALLING

For many years, I believed calling was a destination. I thought it was a title you finally stepped into after enough discipline, enough sacrifice, enough obedience. I viewed it as a platform you earned or a position you reached once you had proven yourself worthy. That mindset was shaped by sports. You grind so you can start. You train so you can move up. You sacrifice so you can reach the next level. Everything feels like a climb toward arrival.

Naturally, I assumed calling with God worked the same way. I believed there would be a moment when I would "arrive" at purpose, as if God were waiting at the finish line to hand me the assignment I had worked for. But over time, especially through failure and rebuilding, I realized I was approaching calling with the wrong lens. Calling is not primarily about where you are going. It is about how you are walking with God right now.

That shift changed everything. Instead of obsessing over position, I began focusing on posture. Instead of chasing platforms, I started prioritizing presence. Instead of asking only what God wanted me to accomplish, I began asking who He wanted me to become. Calling is less about destination and more about direction—less about arrival and more about alignment.

Calling Is Bigger Than a Role

There was a season when I tied calling almost exclusively to assignment. Coach. Leader. Builder. Speaker. Founder. I saw those roles as proof that I was operating in purpose. And while roles matter, I eventually discovered something deeper.

Roles change. Seasons shift. Platforms expand and contract. Doors open and close. But calling remains. Calling is not what you do—it is who you are becoming with God. That distinction is essential if you want lasting purpose rather than temporary significance.

You do not lose your calling when a season ends. You do not forfeit it when a role closes or a door shuts. You do not abandon it when a plan falls apart or when failure interrupts your momentum. If calling disappeared that easily, it was never calling—it was ego attached to outcome.

True calling persists through change. It is refined through challenge. It matures in obscurity as much as it shines in visibility. When your sense of calling is rooted in relationship rather than role, transitions no longer threaten your identity. You remain anchored because your purpose is not limited to a platform. It is sustained by alignment with God.

Why High Performers Confuse Calling and Identity

High achievers are trained early to tie identity to output. Scoreboards measure value. Results determine worth. Wins validate effort. This mindset builds drive, but it can also create fragility. When performance rises, confidence rises. When performance dips, identity feels shaken.

So when we begin talking about calling, our instinctive question often becomes, "What am I supposed to do?" We search for assignment before we consider formation. Yet Jesus approaches it differently. His starting point is, "Who are you becoming?"

Before He assigned responsibility, He cultivated relationship. Before He sent the disciples out, He invited them to walk with Him. Calling flowed from intimacy. It was born from time spent together. Identity preceded mission.

When we confuse calling with identity, we risk measuring our worth by our activity. But authentic calling does not replace relationship—it flows from it. You are not called first to do something impressive. You are called first to belong to Someone transformative.

Understanding this changes how you pursue purpose. It shifts you from striving to abiding. It reminds you that your deepest calling is not found in titles or achievements but in walking faithfully with God. And from that place of rooted identity, the right assignments will emerge at the right time.

Your Calling Will Always Match Your Character

One of the clearest lessons I have learned over time is this: God will never promote you beyond the character you are willing to develop. That truth is not punishment. It is protection. It is the kind of protection that shields you from stepping into responsibility before your foundation can sustain it.

I have watched talented, gifted individuals rise quickly into calling-shaped roles without calling-shaped hearts—and the results are painful. Talent opened the door, but character could not hold the weight. Pressure exposed what formation had not yet secured. When that happens, the fallout affects not only the leader but also everyone connected to them. The devastation is real. And in many cases, it could have been prevented.

Gifting may open opportunities. Character determines longevity. Calling will stretch you, challenge you, and grow you— but it will never require you to abandon the very fruit God is forming in your life. If an opportunity demands that you compromise integrity, sacrifice peace, neglect your family, or override clear obedience, that opportunity is not your calling. It may look impressive. It may feel exciting. But if your soul cannot afford it, it is not aligned.

Maturity means recognizing that not every open door should be walked through. Growth means understanding that depth precedes durability. And durability matters far more than speed. Choosing wisely what you pursue is not weakness. It is wisdom anchored in character.

Clarity Comes in Motion, Not Sitting Out

Another mistake many people make is waiting to feel completely certain before taking action. They want absolute clarity, a full blueprint, or unmistakable confirmation before moving forward. But calling is rarely revealed in stillness alone. It is often discovered in motion.

Direction becomes clearer when you are walking, serving, showing up, and being faithful with what is already in front of you. Waiting for a complete master plan often leads to paralysis. Yet God frequently reveals the next step only after you take the current one.

I did not gain clarity by sitting on the sidelines hoping for a divine download of every future detail. I found clarity by walking daily with God and allowing alignment to shape direction. As I served faithfully in small assignments, larger vision began to emerge naturally. As I honored what was in my hands, confidence grew about what was ahead.

The next step is more important than the full map. Movement guided by faith builds momentum shaped by obedience. When you remain engaged, even in modest responsibilities, purpose unfolds gradually. Motion does not guarantee perfection, but faithfulness in motion cultivates discernment.

Calling Is Discovered in Obedience, Not Ambition

Ambition asks, "How far can I go?" Calling asks, "How faithfully can I walk with God here?" Ambition often chases visibility and advancement. Calling values consistency and faithfulness. Ambition seeks influence quickly. Calling seeks impact that endures.

Ambition rushes. Calling waits. Ambition measures growth by scale. Calling measures growth by depth. There is nothing inherently wrong with ambition; it can drive effort and persistence. But when ambition outruns obedience, it weakens alignment.

The turning point for me came when I stopped chasing platforms and began prioritizing presence. Instead of asking how quickly I could expand, I began asking how faithfully I could steward what was already entrusted to me. Clarity did not appear instantly, but it emerged steadily. The more I pursued relationship, the more direction settled into place.

Purpose is not discovered through force. It is revealed through faithful obedience. When obedience leads, ambition is refined rather than inflated. That refinement strengthens integrity and sharpens focus. And over time, the path ahead becomes clearer—not because you demanded it, but because you walked faithfully into it.

Your Calling Will Always Serve People, Not Just Goals

One of the clearest markers of true calling is this: calling is never self-centered. It is always outward. It always blesses others. And it almost always costs something meaningful. That cost might be time, comfort, ego, convenience, or control, but real calling will stretch you beyond self-preservation. If what you call "calling" only benefits you—your image, your platform, your bank account, or your reputation—then it's not calling. It's ambition dressed up in spiritual language.

Jesus makes this unmistakably clear. He did not step into purpose for recognition. He stepped into sacrifice. He didn't pursue a platform to be celebrated; He carried a cross to love people. His example demands our attention because it confronts the version of calling that is centered on self-advancement. Calling does not exist to elevate you. It exists to love people well through you. When you embrace that truth, your perspective shifts. You stop asking, "How does this grow me?" and start asking, "Who does this serve?" You stop measuring purpose by applause and start measuring it by impact.

And here's what I've seen time and again: when your calling is rooted in serving people, your influence becomes healthier, your motivation becomes purer, and your impact multiplies in ways you could never manufacture. Purpose fueled by love is always stronger than purpose fueled by ego.

Seasons Shape Calling

Calling doesn't usually arrive all at once. It unfolds in layers, often through seasons you would never choose but later come to deeply value. There are preparation seasons where God strengthens foundations. There are hidden seasons where identity is secured without the pressure of visibility. There are correction seasons where motives are purified and direction is adjusted. There are stretching seasons where you grow beyond comfort and learn endurance. And there are release seasons where opportunities expand and fruit becomes more visible.

The key is this: you don't skip stages. You don't rush timing. You don't bypass formation. Each phase carries something irreplaceable. If you skip the hidden season, you often build identity on approval. If you avoid correction, you repeat patterns that eventually sabotage progress. If you rush release, you carry weight you aren't ready to steward. God loves you too much to accelerate you beyond what your character can sustain.

God cares more about who you become in the process than how impressive the final outcome looks. That truth has anchored me in seasons that felt slow, quiet, and even frustrating. If you trust Him with the process, He will handle the purpose with perfect timing. Your job is faithfulness. His job is fruit.

Reflection

Where have you tied your calling too tightly to a role, a title, or a specific outcome? Consider whether you've connected purpose to a position rather than to a posture. Sometimes the thing we think we're called to do is simply the vehicle God uses to shape who we are called to become. Sit with that question long enough to let it reveal what's really driving you.

Heart Check

Are you chasing clarity—or walking faithfully with Jesus right where you are? It's a simple question, but it reveals a lot. Faithfulness often looks ordinary, but it is the soil where calling grows. If you're waiting to feel "ready" before you obey, you may be delaying the very process that produces readiness.

Simple Action Step

Ask Jesus this question sincerely: "Who are You calling me to become before You show me what You want me to do?" Then pay attention—not primarily to titles, opportunities, or roles, but to character. Notice where He is shaping humility, patience, courage, purity, integrity, and love.

True calling is not something you achieve like a trophy. It is something you live—one faithful step at a time. Don't wait for the perfect moment. Start today by obeying what you already know, serving who is already in front of you, and becoming the kind of person who can carry purpose with health and grace.

CHAPTER 15

MY RELATIONSHIP HAS STRENGTHENED MY FAITH AND FOCUS

Before I truly learned how to walk with Jesus, my faith felt scattered—and so did my focus. I believed in God. I respected Scripture. I knew the stories and could speak the language. But if I'm honest, my life had no real spiritual center. My faith existed, but it wasn't anchoring anything.

As an athlete and later as a coach, I was trained to lock in on results. Focus meant tunnel vision. Block out distractions. Grind harder. Push through pain. Win at all costs. That mindset produced measurable results on the field. It built discipline, intensity, and resilience. But internally, it left me fractured. I was spiritually undisciplined because my focus was rooted in outcomes, not in intimacy with God.

When my relationship with Jesus became real—not theoretical, not performative—something shifted at the core of how I lived, trained, and led. My faith stopped feeling fragile. My focus stopped feeling forced. Not because life became easier or smoother, but because my foundation finally grew deeper and stronger. I wasn't trying to manufacture stability anymore. I was anchored in it.

Faith That Doesn't Collapse Under Pressure

Before relationship, my faith was heavily tied to circumstances. When things were going well, I felt confident. When doors opened and results showed up, I assumed God was close. But when things fell apart, when pressure mounted or outcomes disappointed, I felt distant—sometimes even abandoned.

If pressure increased, I tried harder. If failure hit, I withdrew. Looking back, that wasn't faith. It was emotional management tied to performance. My confidence rose and fell with my environment because my trust wasn't deeply rooted.

Real faith doesn't come from simply understanding theology better. It comes from trust built through daily relationship. Walking with Jesus consistently—especially in private, when no one sees— gave my faith weight. It gave it substance. I wasn't just agreeing with truths; I was experiencing them.

That kind of faith doesn't evaporate when the scoreboard flips or a season ends unexpectedly. It doesn't panic when momentum stalls. Faith became something I stood on, not something I occasionally visited. It became a steady presence rather than a situational reaction. And that stability changed how I handled both victory and loss.

Focus Wasn't About Control—It Was About Alignment

For most of my career, I believed focus meant control. Control the outcome. Control the narrative. Control my image. Control my future. That type of focus feels powerful, but it is incredibly exhausting—and ultimately fragile. The moment something slips beyond your control, anxiety floods in.

Relationship with Jesus reframed focus entirely. I learned that true focus isn't about tightening your grip; it's about aligning your heart. Alignment over control. When you're aligned with Jesus, decisions grow clearer. Distractions lose their dominance. Anxiety loosens its grip. Priorities begin to reorder themselves without constant striving.

I didn't become less driven. I became rightly driven. My motivation shifted from self-protection to surrendered partnership. I stopped obsessing over what I needed to defend or secure and started asking a better question: Who am I walking with in this moment?

That question recalibrated my leadership, my marriage, my fatherhood, and my calling. Focus no longer meant forcing outcomes. It meant staying aligned with the One who holds them. And in that alignment, faith and clarity strengthened together— quietly, steadily, powerfully.

Private Time With God Refined My Inner Game

Every serious athlete understands a foundational truth: games are won long before game day. They're won in the quiet reps no one applauds. In the early mornings when no one is watching. In the repetitive drills that feel boring but build precision. In the disciplined habits that shape instinct over time. Championships are rarely decided under the lights—they're prepared in obscurity.

My faith and focus strengthened the same way. It wasn't the sermons I heard or the stages I stood on that rebuilt me. It wasn't public spirituality or visible leadership moments. It was private prayer—honest, unfiltered, unperformed—that became my real training ground.

In those quiet moments with Jesus, something deeper was formed. That's where clarity took shape. That's where temptation slowly began losing its leverage. That's where confidence was restored—not confidence in myself, but confidence in who I was walking with. That's where peace began replacing the constant internal pressure I had normalized for years.

Private time with God refined my inner game. It exposed blind spots. It corrected motives. It strengthened discernment. It reminded me daily that leadership begins within before it ever reaches others. You don't drift into spiritual focus. You train into it—deliberately, consistently, and humbly. Just like athletics, the unseen work determines the visible result.

Faith Anchors Focus When Emotions Are Loud

High performers feel deeply—even when they pretend they don't. We feel pressure intensely. We carry fear of failure quietly. We sense expectations constantly. We compare more than we admit. We wrestle with uncertainty beneath confident exteriors. Emotions may not always show outwardly, but they shape decisions internally if left unchecked.

Before relationship, my emotions often ran the show. If I felt confident, I acted boldly. If I felt threatened, I tightened control. If I felt discouraged, I pulled back. Decisions were driven by emotional spikes rather than steady conviction.

After relationship became central, emotions still showed up— but they no longer had authority. They informed me, but they didn't rule me. Faith became the anchor. Focus followed. When relationship defined my pace instead of feelings defining my reactions, leadership grew steadier. My responses slowed down. My reactions softened. My decisions carried more discernment and less defensiveness.

The noise inside quieted. Not because emotions disappeared, but because trust grew stronger than impulse. Leadership felt less chaotic internally. Life felt less fragile beneath the surface. Faith anchored focus in a way ambition never could.

Faith Gives Focus Its Endurance

Motivation fades. Emotions fluctuate. Circumstances shift unexpectedly. Seasons change. Criticism comes. Momentum stalls. If your focus is built on adrenaline or temporary excitement, it won't last long under sustained pressure.

But relationship sustains focus when motivation disappears. That's endurance. The same way conditioning allows an athlete to finish strong in the fourth quarter when others are exhausted, relationship with Jesus builds spiritual stamina. It keeps you steady when you're misunderstood. It keeps you grounded in losing streaks. It stabilizes you in delayed seasons and protects you when uncertainty rises.

I didn't lose intensity. I gained sustainability. That shift changed everything. Intensity without endurance burns out. Intensity with alignment transforms. My drive remained, but it was no longer fueled by insecurity or pressure. It was sustained by trust.

And that kind of focus doesn't just improve performance—it restores peace. It allows you to lead long-term without collapsing under the weight. It keeps you moving forward when others suggest you step back. Faith gave my focus endurance. And endurance gave my leadership depth that pressure alone never could.

Faith and Focus Feed Each Other

Faith without focus can become passive. It sounds spiritual, but it drifts. It believes good things, yet lacks direction. On the other hand, focus without faith becomes frantic. It chases results, manages optics, and pushes relentlessly—but it eventually runs out of fuel. I've lived on both sides of that tension.

What I've learned is this: faith and focus were never meant to compete. They are designed to feed each other. When faith is rooted in authentic relationship with Jesus, focus becomes clear and purposeful. It sharpens. Distractions that once felt urgent start to fade into background noise. Energy is no longer scattered across meaningless pursuits—it is stewarded intentionally. Leadership grows steady and visionary instead of reactive and chaotic.

Faith reminds you who you are and whose you are. It grounds identity. Focus then becomes the daily expression of that identity. Instead of trying to prove yourself, you begin leading and living from a place of alignment. You don't wake up asking how to protect your image—you wake up asking how to remain faithful. That shift is subtle, but it is powerful.

When faith anchors you, focus stops being about control. It becomes about conviction. You stop hustling for validation and start walking with clarity. And clarity always outperforms chaos. The more my relationship deepened, the more my attention refined. What once drained me lost its pull. What truly mattered gained priority. Faith stabilized the foundation. Focus built on top of it with strength and endurance.

Reflection

Where has pressure scattered your focus recently? Be honest. Have expectations, deadlines, or fear quietly pulled your attention away from what truly matters? What would change in your leadership, your marriage, your parenting, your calling—if relationship, not results, became the center again?

Heart Check

Is your focus being driven by fear and control—or by alignment and trust? One produces anxiety and constant tension. The other produces steadiness and quiet confidence. Look at the fruit in your life right now. Which foundation is actually shaping your decisions?

Simple Action Step

Start each morning this week with one simple but powerful question in prayer: "Jesus, what actually matters today?" Write the answer down. Protect it. Guard it from unnecessary distractions. Let relationship shape your focus before the world tries to define it for you.

Because when your relationship is strong, your faith stabilizes. And when your faith is steady, your focus follows with clarity that no pressure can shake.

CHAPTER 16

ALIGNMENT OVER ADRENALINE

For most of my life, I mistook adrenaline for purpose. That confusion shaped my decisions, my leadership style, and my identity more than I realized—and it nearly cost me everything that actually mattered. As an athlete, adrenaline was fuel. It sharpened my instincts and heightened my awareness. As a coach, it felt like momentum—the emotional surge that kept me driving forward. As a leader, it felt like life itself. The crowds, the pressure, the deadlines, the competition, the next opportunity, the next deal, the next win—those spikes of energy made me feel alive and productive.

Adrenaline kept me sharp, but it never kept me whole. It pushed me forward with relentless intensity, but it never grounded me in peace. Over time, living at that pace began to wear me down. Spiritually, I was inconsistent. Emotionally, I was volatile. Relationally, I was distracted. From the outside, things often looked impressive. Internally, I was exhausted. I didn't realize that what I

173

called passion was often pressure—and what I called drive was sometimes just dependency on the next high.

Adrenaline Is a Short-Term Motivator

Adrenaline is powerful, but it is temporary. It spikes in big moments and convinces you that you can sustain that pace forever. Then it fades in the quiet moments and leaves you depleted. It thrives in chaos, which subtly trains you to crave busyness and urgency. And when stillness comes, it feels uncomfortable—almost threatening—because there's no rush to carry you.

I became skilled at living off adrenaline. My calendar was packed with impossibly tight schedules. Expectations were often unrealistic, but I justified them as commitment. Urgency was constant, sometimes even manufactured. I remained perpetually "on," always proving, always pushing. And externally, it looked like productivity. It looked disciplined. It looked ambitious.

But internally, something was eroding. The pace that produced short-term wins was quietly draining long-term strength. You can win games on adrenaline. You cannot build a meaningful, sustainable life on it. A life fueled only by intensity will eventually collapse under its own weight.

Religion Feeds Adrenaline

Here's a truth that many avoid acknowledging: some religious systems unintentionally reward adrenaline. More services. More events. More activity. More urgency in the name of devotion. More visibility mistaken for faithfulness. It can create the illusion of spiritual growth while quietly disconnecting you from intimacy with God.

I stayed busy in those environments. Exhausted, but active. Involved, but not anchored. I was doing things "for God" without consistently being with Him. Religion gave me routines and responsibilities, but it didn't automatically produce rhythm. My calendar was full, but my soul often wasn't.

Relationship changed that. Relationship introduced life-giving rhythm where religion had emphasized relentless movement. It taught me that consistency matters more than intensity. That intimacy outweighs image. That presence is stronger than performance. Rhythm sustains what adrenaline only spikes temporarily.

Alignment Is Slower—but Infinitely Stronger

When my relationship with Jesus shifted from obligation to authenticity, something began to recalibrate. Life didn't become passive—it became purposeful. The noise softened. Artificial urgency lost its grip. Clarity increased, not because ambition disappeared, but because alignment replaced adrenaline.

Alignment asks better questions. Is this God-led or ego-driven? Am I responding thoughtfully or reacting emotionally? Is this sustainable or just impressive for the moment? Is this drawing me closer to Jesus or simply feeding momentum for momentum's sake? Those questions slowed me down at first. And for a high achiever, slowing down can feel uncomfortable—even threatening.

But alignment builds strength that adrenaline never can. It doesn't rush. It doesn't panic. It doesn't compete needlessly. It listens. It discerns. It waits when necessary. And over time, you realize that waiting is not weakness—it is wisdom in motion.

Adrenaline excites. Alignment endures. Adrenaline surges. Alignment sustains. When you learn to value alignment over adrenaline, your leadership becomes steadier, your relationships deepen, and your soul finally finds a pace it can live at for the long run.

Jesus Never Led From Adrenaline

When you study the life of Jesus closely, one thing becomes unmistakably clear: He never led from adrenaline. And if anyone had a reason to feel rushed, it was Him.

Crowds constantly pressed in for more. The sick needed healing. The broken needed hope. Religious leaders questioned, criticized, and tried to trap Him. Even His closest disciples misunderstood Him repeatedly. Human need surrounded Him without pause. Deadlines were real. The mission was urgent. The cross was coming.

And yet—He was never frantic. Never reactive. Never driven by chaos.

He withdrew deliberately. He prayed intimately. He waited patiently. He moved according to divine timing, not human urgency. When people tried to accelerate Him, He slowed down. When they tried to define His agenda, He aligned with the Father instead. That is perfect alignment.

If the Son of God, carrying the most significant mission in history, did not lead from adrenaline—why do we convince ourselves that we must? Why do we assume constant urgency is spiritual maturity? Why do we equate busyness with obedience? Jesus modeled something radically different. He demonstrated that calm confidence under pressure is not weakness. It is alignment.

Adrenaline Feels Powerful—Alignment Creates True Peace

Adrenaline feels strong in the moment. It heightens your senses. It amplifies emotion. It creates temporary intensity that mimics purpose. But it cannot sustain you. It demands more and more to keep producing the same effect.

Alignment, on the other hand, is quieter—but infinitely stronger.

Adrenaline gives you intensity. Alignment gives you peace.

Adrenaline creates fleeting momentum. Alignment establishes clear direction.

Adrenaline anxiously asks, "What's next?" Alignment confidently asks, "What's right?"

When I chose alignment over adrenaline, I didn't lose my competitive edge. I didn't suddenly become passive or complacent. What I lost was unnecessary pressure. I lost the constant need to prove, to rush, to react. I lost the anxiety that came from trying to hold everything together in my own strength.

And here's the truth: that pressure was never producing authentic power anyway. It was producing stress disguised as strength. Alignment replaced that with something deeper—steady conviction, clarity under pressure, and peace in the middle of responsibility. And peace is far more powerful than hype.

Leadership Inevitably Breaks When Adrenaline Leads

This was one of the hardest lessons I had to face as both a coach and a leader. Adrenaline-driven leadership eventually breaks something—if not the leader, then the team.

Adrenaline-driven leaders tend to react emotionally instead of responding wisely. They overcommit themselves and everyone around them. They create environments where urgency becomes culture. They blur boundaries between work and life. They confuse what is loud with what is important.

On the surface, it can look impressive. Fast decisions. High output. Constant movement. But underneath, people feel the weight. Burnout creeps in. Trust weakens. Creativity dries up. The pace becomes unsustainable.

Alignment-driven leaders look different. They respond thoughtfully, even when pressure rises. They choose commitments carefully. They protect their teams from unnecessary exhaustion. They honor healthy rhythms and boundaries. They lead with clarity rather than chaos.

Teams don't need leaders high on adrenaline. They need leaders grounded in alignment. They need someone steady enough to filter noise, wise enough to protect pace, and humble enough to stay aligned with God's timing. Because when alignment leads, pressure no longer controls the culture—peace does.

Private Alignment Fuels Public Clarity

Alignment is not built on a stage, in a boardroom, or in the middle of high-pressure meetings. It is built in sacred solitude—quiet places where there is no applause, no urgency to perform, and no need to prove anything. That is where real leadership is formed. In my life, alignment has come through focused prayer, honest self-reflection, and the kind of stillness that forces you to face what's actually driving you. It is choosing to sit with God before making decisions, rather than rushing to act just to relieve pressure. It is listening without demanding predetermined outcomes, and staying present long enough for wisdom to rise.

That private work is where adrenaline slowly loses its grip. It is where the noise quiets down and discernment becomes clearer. I've learned that when I am deeply aligned with Jesus in private, I feel far less need to manufacture urgency in public. I don't have to fill every silence with words. I don't have to force momentum to feel effective. Clarity begins to show up not because life becomes simpler, but because my spirit becomes steadier. Public leadership becomes stronger when private alignment is consistent.

You Don't Need Less Passion—You Need Better Direction

This chapter is not asking you to slow down for comfort's sake. It is inviting you to redirect your fire toward what actually matters. Many high-capacity people don't need more motivation—they need clearer direction. Passion is not the problem. Misalignment is. Adrenaline can make you feel powerful while quietly pulling you away from peace. Alignment does the opposite. It doesn't kill drive—it disciplines it. It concentrates energy instead of scattering it. It turns raw intensity into sustainable leadership.

Alignment replaces draining chaos with empowering clarity. It trades distracting noise for genuine authority. It does not remove ambition; it refines it. And when ambition is refined by relationship with Jesus, it becomes a force for lasting impact rather than a frantic chase for the next high. You still move forward. You still lead decisively. But you do it with steadiness instead of strain, and with wisdom instead of impulse. That kind of leadership lasts. It builds teams without breaking souls. It creates progress without sacrificing peace.

Reflection

Where in your life are you currently operating on depleting adrenaline instead of life-giving alignment? Consider what areas feel frantic, pressured, or constantly urgent. Ask yourself what you are afraid will happen if you slow down. Often, that fear reveals where adrenaline has been functioning as a substitute for trust.

Heart Check

Are your most important decisions being driven by artificial urgency—or by thoughtful discernment? Do you feel pushed, rushed, and reactive, or settled, clear, and aligned? The pace and tone of your decision-making often reveal what is fueling your leadership beneath the surface.

Simple Action Step

Before your next major decision, pause intentionally and pray, "Jesus, am I truly aligned with Your purposes—or just activated by pressure?" Then wait. Listen. Resist the instinct to force an answer or rush to action. Choose alignment over adrenaline deliberately.

Adrenaline fades. Alignment endures. And leadership built on authentic alignment will carry you further than intensity ever could—because it is rooted in peace, strengthened by wisdom, and sustained by the presence of God.

CHAPTER 17

GRATEFUL FOR HIS MERCY, GRACE, AND SECOND CHANCES

There are few words that carry more weight in my life today than mercy and grace. These aren't just theological terms I learned in church. They are not abstract ideas or polished phrases used in sermons. They are the lived reality of my story. They are the reason I am still standing.

If my journey makes anything clear, it is this: I am not here because I held everything together. I am not standing because of my discipline, my intelligence, or my strength. I am standing because God, in His compassion, refused to walk away from me—even when I had made choices that could have justified it. That realization humbles me every time I revisit it. Mercy and grace are no longer distant doctrines. They are the foundation beneath my feet.

I Needed Mercy Before I Understood Grace

For a long time, I didn't think I needed mercy. I convinced myself I just needed more focus, more drive, more forward momentum. I justified decisions that slowly drifted me off course. I ignored conviction because it felt inconvenient. I outran uncomfortable truths by staying busy. I covered wounds with visible success.

On the outside, everything looked solid. The career moved forward. The leadership roles expanded. The image held. But internally, things were cracking. I was exhausted in places no one could see. I was compartmentalizing parts of my life just to keep functioning. Eventually, the pace stopped working. The distractions stopped numbing. The consequences of my choices caught up to me.

Rock bottom wasn't dramatic or explosive. It was honest. Painfully honest. I was tired of pretending. Tired of managing. Tired of carrying weight I was never meant to hold. That is where mercy found me. Not with a lecture. Not with humiliation. Not with a spotlight on my failure. Mercy met me with rescue when I had run out of excuses.

Mercy Is God Not Giving You What You Deserve

Looking back, I know my decisions could have cost me far more than they did. They could have cost me my family. They could have destroyed my credibility completely. They could have derailed my calling permanently. By human standards, I deserved fallout. I deserved separation. I deserved to reap the full weight of my choices.

But mercy intervened.

God did not pretend my sin was harmless. He confronted it. He brought it into the light. He corrected me. But He refused to abandon me inside it. He disciplined me without crushing me. He exposed the problem without erasing the possibility of redemption. That is mercy. Mercy does not deny consequences—but it tempers them with compassion. It does not ignore accountability—but it leaves room for restoration.

I deserved isolation. He offered presence. I deserved rejection. He extended patience. That is the gift of mercy—undeserved restraint rooted in love.

Grace Is God Giving You What You Didn't Earn

If mercy kept me from losing everything, grace carried me forward into something new. Grace did more than pull me out of the pit. It invited me to walk again. Not as a project under supervision. Not as a second-tier believer. Not as someone permanently disqualified from meaningful impact.

Grace spoke differently than my shame did. Where shame whispered that I had wasted my opportunity, grace declared that my story wasn't finished. Where fear suggested permanent sidelining, grace reminded me that calling flows from relationship, not perfection.

I expected distance. God offered restoration. I anticipated limited trust. He extended fresh responsibility at the right time. Religion might have labeled me by my worst chapter. Grace rewrote the narrative through repentance and surrender.

Grace does not erase history. It redeems it. It does not pretend failure didn't happen. It transforms it into wisdom and humility. And because of that grace, I lead differently now. I speak differently. I live differently. Not because I'm proud of my mistakes—but because I am deeply grateful for the second chance I did not earn.

Mercy kept me from being destroyed by my past. Grace gave me courage to step into my future. And both continue to shape who I am becoming every single day.

Second Chances Are the Language of the Gospel

One of the most devastating lies we tend to believe after failure is painfully simple: "You had your chance, and you blew it." That voice can sound convincing. It can feel final. It can convince you that one mistake—or one season of mistakes—has permanently disqualified you from anything meaningful.

But that is not the language of Jesus.

Peter denied Him three times, publicly and painfully. David failed in ways that shook a nation. Paul persecuted the very church he would later build. And I self-destructed in quieter ways— compromises, pride, ego, drift. Yet none of them were finished in God's story. Not Peter. Not David. Not Paul. Not me.

And not you.

Second chances are not rare exceptions in God's economy. They are the pattern of His grace. The Gospel itself is built on restoration. The cross was not a statement of disqualification—it was an invitation to return. When Jesus restores, He does not merely tolerate you. He reassigns you. He does not reduce you to your worst chapter. He rewrites the narrative through surrender and transformation.

Second chances are not sentimental. They are powerful. They are not cheap. They are costly—paid for with mercy and sustained by grace. And they remind us that failure may interrupt your journey, but it does not erase your calling.

Grace Doesn't Remove Consequences—It Redeems Them

Grace does not mean the absence of consequences. That is an important truth. After my collapse, I had hard conversations. I had to rebuild trust patiently. I had to confront pride I had ignored for too long. I had to learn patience in seasons that did not move at my speed.

There were uncomfortable moments. There were humbling realities. There were things I could not undo. But grace met me in those consequences and began to redeem them.

Where shame could have buried me permanently, grace rebuilt me steadily. Where failure could have defined me forever, grace refined me instead. It exposed what needed healing without condemning me to hopelessness. It used pain as a teacher rather than a jailer.

Grace doesn't say consequences don't matter. It says they don't get the final word. It transforms regret into humility. It turns embarrassment into empathy. It converts brokenness into wisdom. And over time, you begin to see that the very things that once threatened to end you can become the tools God uses to deepen you.

You Lead Differently When You Know You've Been Forgiven

Mercy changed the way I see myself. Grace changed the way I see others. When you know you've been forgiven—truly forgiven—it shifts your leadership at the core.

You begin to lead with compassion instead of constant critique. You correct without crushing. You restore instead of replace. You protect hearts as much as performance. You understand that people are more than their worst mistake, because you know you are.

Leaders who forget mercy often demand rigid perfection. They lead from insecurity and pressure. But leaders who live from grace create environments where growth is possible. They allow room for learning. They hold standards without weaponizing shame. They remember how it felt to be rescued.

I no longer lead to prove my value. I don't lead to compensate for my past. I lead from gratitude. From the overflow of knowing I was given a second chance I did not earn. And when you lead from gratitude instead of guilt, everything changes.

Because forgiven leaders don't build cultures of fear. They build cultures of freedom, accountability, and hope.

Gratitude Is the Fruit of Grace

One of the clearest changes in my life since truly experiencing mercy and grace is this: my obedience is no longer rooted in fear. I don't follow Jesus because I'm terrified of punishment. I follow Him because I am profoundly grateful. That difference reshapes everything.

I don't serve to earn His approval. I serve because I already have it. I don't pray to secure favor. I pray because I've been given favor I could never earn. Gratitude fuels a kind of consistency that fear never could. Fear may motivate short-term compliance, but gratitude produces long-term faithfulness. When motivation fades, gratitude remains. When hardship stretches you, gratitude sustains you. When pride tries to creep back in, gratitude humbles you gently and keeps your heart soft.

Every morning, I am reminded of something simple but powerful: I did not earn this restored life. I did not deserve this renewed calling. I did not manufacture this redemption story. God intervened. God restored. God rebuilt. That daily awareness grounds me. It protects me from entitlement and keeps my heart aligned with humility.

Gratitude is not passive emotion. It is active perspective. It shifts how I lead, how I speak, how I make decisions. It reminds me that everything I have is a gift, and every opportunity to serve is grace in motion.

If God Gave Me Another Chance, He Can Give You One Too

If you're carrying regret right now—deep, heavy, suffocating regret—I understand. If you feel like you've gone too far, damaged too much, or waited too long, I understand. If your past feels louder than your future, or if shame keeps replaying your failures like a relentless highlight reel, I understand that too.

But here's what I need you to hear clearly: grace is not fragile. It does not run out because you ran far. Mercy is not scarce. It is not rationed or reserved for the "less messy." Second chances are not rare exceptions in God's story. They are the essence of it.

Jesus does not specialize in disqualification. He specializes in restoration. He does not look at your worst decision and declare you finished. He looks at surrendered hearts and begins rebuilding. If He met me in my mess and brought me through it, He can meet you in yours. If He restored my calling after I nearly sabotaged it, He can restore hope in you.

Your past may explain part of your story, but it does not get to define its ending.

Reflection

Where have you struggled to believe that God could still use you powerfully despite your failures? Take a moment to identify the specific regret that keeps surfacing. Naming it honestly is often the first step toward breaking its hold.

Heart Check

Are you living like someone who is truly forgiven—or just someone who believes forgiveness exists in theory? There is a difference between knowing about grace and walking in it. One keeps you cautious and distant. The other fills you with confidence and peace.

Simple Action Step

Today, pray this honestly: "Jesus, help me live confidently from grace, not crippled by shame." Then pause and thank Him—specifically. Thank Him for mercy that spared you. For grace that restored you. For the second chance you are standing in right now.

Because your story is not over. It is being redeemed in ways you may not even see yet. And no matter what chapter you are in, grace always—without exception—gets the final word.

CHAPTER 18

FOLLOWING THE CALLING: PLANTING SEEDS, POINTING TO JESUS

At some point after God rebuilt my life, the core question began to shift. It was no longer, "What do I want to do?" That question had driven me for years. It had fueled ambition, shaped decisions, and justified relentless pace. But after experiencing mercy and restoration, something deeper took hold. The question became, "What did He rescue me to do?"

That change was not dramatic or instantaneous. It did not arrive like a lightning bolt that suddenly illuminated my entire future. Instead, it became clearer through obedience. Through prayer that was honest and sometimes uncomfortable. Through reflection that forced me to confront motives. Through alignment that required me to slow down and listen. Over time, a powerful realization emerged: God was not asking me to abandon my world. He was inviting me to redeem it.

He did not remove my passion for sports. He refined it. He did not erase my leadership instincts. He reshaped them. He did not eliminate my drive. He redirected it. Calling did not mean starting over in a completely different arena. It meant stepping back into familiar spaces with a transformed heart and a new lens.

Calling Isn't a Platform—It's a Direction

For years, I believed calling meant reaching a certain platform. A title. A role. A recognized lane you fought to earn and defend. I measured calling by visibility and influence. But over time, I've come to understand that calling is both simpler and infinitely more profound.

Calling is directional, not positional. It is not about where you stand—it is about where your life consistently points people. A platform can amplify impact, but it does not define it. Direction does. My calling is not to make people admire my résumé. It is to help them see Jesus more clearly through how I live, lead, and speak.

Sometimes that looks bold and public. Sometimes it is quiet and personal. Sometimes it happens in a conversation after practice. Sometimes it unfolds in a classroom discussion. But it is always intentional. Always relational. Always anchored in pointing beyond myself.

When you understand calling this way, you stop obsessing over visibility. You begin focusing on alignment. You ask less about how high you can climb and more about how faithfully you can walk.

Sports Were Never the Point—They Were the Mission Field

Sports shaped me in ways I will always respect. They built discipline in early mornings and long practices. They exposed my ego in both winning and losing. They taught endurance when quitting felt easier. They revealed the power of teamwork, sacrifice, and focus. Athletics trained me in ways that no classroom could.

But sports were never meant to be my ultimate identity. They were my assignment. They were the environment where God formed me—and then sent me back in with purpose.

Athletes understand pressure. They live in the tension between expectation and performance. They embrace the grind. They feel the weight of failure and the surge of victory. Few environments reveal character like a locker room does. That is why I now see sports as one of the most fertile mission fields available.

I do not preach at athletes from a distance. I walk alongside them. I train them with excellence. I mentor them through adversity. I speak truth in moments that matter. And through both example and conversation, I point them toward Jesus—not as a rigid system of rules, but as a relationship that anchors identity beyond the scoreboard.

Sports are not the end goal. They are the context. The platform is temporary. The impact on a soul is eternal.

Education Became a Place of Formation, Not Just Information

Alongside sports, God placed a burden on my heart for education—not merely degrees or credentials, but formation. I began to see how many gifted individuals were externally accomplished but internally unstable. How many leaders achieved impressive milestones while quietly struggling with emptiness. How many students mastered information without developing identity.

Education, when aligned with calling, becomes far more than academic advancement. It becomes formation. It shapes character. It strengthens discernment. It builds resilience. It teaches people how to think critically, live intentionally, and lead responsibly.

When education is infused with purpose, it does not just prepare students for careers. It prepares them for life. It plants seeds of integrity and faith that outlast semesters and syllabi. In classrooms and mentoring environments, I have seen how consistent investment can redirect a trajectory.

I am not called to build impressive institutions for reputation's sake. I am called to cultivate environments where people grow—intellectually, emotionally, and spiritually. Where questions are welcomed. Where identity is strengthened. Where Jesus is not forced, but faithfully represented.

Planting seeds and pointing to Jesus may not always trend publicly. But it is powerful. It is lasting. And it is the kind of calling that multiplies quietly over time—one life, one conversation, one act of obedience at a time.

Speaking Isn't About Applause—It's About Alignment

Motivational speaking placed a microphone in my hand, but relationship with Jesus placed responsibility in my heart. Early on, it was easy to enjoy the energy of a crowd, the engagement, the response. Applause can feel affirming. Momentum can feel powerful. But over time, I realized something critical: if I only spoke to excite people, I would leave them inspired for a moment and unchanged for a lifetime.

Now, when I step onto a stage, I carry a different weight. I do not speak simply to create hype. I speak to anchor hearts in truth. I do not aim for emotional spikes. I aim for alignment. Words have influence, and influence demands integrity. Every audience deserves authenticity. Every message carries an opportunity—not to elevate my accomplishments—but to point clearly toward Jesus and the lasting transformation He offers.

Sometimes that direction is explicit. Sometimes it is subtle. But it is always intentional. When speaking flows from alignment rather than ego, the goal shifts. The applause matters less. The impact matters more. The stage becomes stewardship, not spotlight. And leadership becomes service, not performance.

Books Are Seeds I May Never See Fully Grow

Writing entered my journey almost unexpectedly, yet it has become one of the most meaningful expressions of my calling. Books function differently than speeches. They do not demand immediate response. They invite reflection. They sit quietly, waiting for the right moment in someone's life.

A book may be opened during a crisis, during a season of doubt, or during a quiet search for meaning. It may travel farther than I ever will. It may reach someone I will never meet. That is both humbling and powerful. Written words become seeds planted beyond direct control.

There is something deeply encouraging about knowing that a message can meet someone privately, without pressure, without an audience. Books create space for people to wrestle with ideas at their own pace. They allow hearts to soften without spotlight. I may never witness the full fruit of those seeds—but God will. And that truth frees me from needing to see the results to trust the process.

Seed Planters Don't Control the Harvest

One of the greatest freedoms I have discovered in embracing my calling is this: I am not responsible for the harvest. I do not have to persuade every skeptic. I do not have to generate instant transformation. I do not have to manage outcomes beyond my assignment.

My role is to plant faithfully. God's role is to grow powerfully.

Authentic calling is not about obsessively measuring visible success. It is about placing truth carefully, consistently, and courageously in the soil of people's lives. Some seeds take root immediately and flourish. Others remain hidden for years before breaking through. Some may grow in ways I never witness.

That is not failure. That is faith.

When you release control of the harvest, you gain peace in the planting. You serve without striving. You speak without forcing.

You write without demanding applause. You trust that obedience matters more than immediate results.

Planting seeds and pointing to Jesus may not always look dramatic. But over time, it builds something far more meaningful than hype—it cultivates lasting transformation rooted in alignment, sustained by grace, and multiplied far beyond what one life alone could produce.

Pointing to Jesus Is the Through Line

When I step back and look at my life—sports, education, speaking, writing—I see different lanes of influence. Different environments. Different audiences. Different tools. But the direction has become the same.

There is one through line that connects it all: pointing to Jesus.

Whether I'm in a locker room, a classroom, on a stage, or behind a keyboard, the goal has shifted. I no longer measure success by applause, growth metrics, or even visible outcomes. I measure it by something quieter but far more powerful. Did this moment, this message, this interaction move someone even one step closer to seeing Jesus clearly?

Because knowing about Jesus intellectually is not remotely the same as knowing Him personally. I knew about Him for years. I knew the stories. I knew the language. I knew the theology. But I didn't truly walk with Him. And that difference changes everything.

If people walk away impressed with my résumé, my experience, or my speaking ability, I've missed it. If they leave motivated but not anchored, I've aimed too low. But if they leave curious about

Him—if a question lingers, if a seed settles, if their heart softens toward relationship—then something eternal has begun.

That is the through line. Not platform. Not performance. Direction.

You Don't Need a New Life—You Need Alignment

If you're wrestling with your calling right now, feeling uncertain or behind, let me offer you something freeing: God is not asking you to become someone entirely different. He is inviting you to align what you already carry with His greater purpose.

Your hard-earned skills matter. Your story matters. Your past pain matters. The lessons you learned in failure, the discipline you built in success, the relationships you've cultivated, the platforms you stand on—all of it can be redeemed. Nothing is wasted when surrendered.

Calling is rarely about replacement. It's about redemption. God didn't erase my love for sports. He redefined its purpose. He didn't remove my leadership instincts. He refined their direction. He didn't silence my voice. He aligned it.

You don't need a new personality. You need alignment. You don't need a dramatic reinvention. You need surrender. When your life is aligned, your existing gifts become instruments of impact. The same lanes, the same circles, the same opportunities—now infused with eternal meaning.

Reflection

Where has God already placed you to plant seeds in the lives of others? Look at your daily environment. Your team. Your workplace. Your family. Your friendships. Your influence may be closer than you think. Calling often hides in the ordinary.

Heart Check

Are you striving to build something impressive for God—or are you learning to walk closely with Him while you build? There is a difference. One is fueled by ego. The other is sustained by intimacy. One seeks visibility. The other seeks faithfulness.

Simple Action Step

Today, ask Jesus this direct question: "Where do You want me to plant seeds right now?" Then pay attention. Not to what looks loud or impressive. Not to what seems biggest. Pay attention to direction. To opportunity. To the people already in front of you.

True calling is not about being widely known. It is about being deeply faithful. And faithfulness has a way of multiplying quietly, steadily, and far beyond what we can see.

CHAPTER 19

FINISH THE RACE THE RIGHT WAY

Every champion athlete understands a simple but powerful truth: it's not how you start—it's how you finish. I've seen athletes with extraordinary talent burn out because they couldn't endure the grind. I've watched underdogs, overlooked and underestimated, outlast favorites because they stayed disciplined, humble, and focused when others faded. Over the years, I've lived on both sides of that reality.

And what I've learned is this: finishing well requires more than talent. It requires endurance.

This book was never about quick spiritual wins or emotional spikes. It was about building a relationship with Jesus that carries you for the long haul. Real faith is not a sprint fueled by hype. It is a lifelong journey of obedience built on trust. It's showing up consistently when feelings fluctuate. It's staying aligned when circumstances shift. It's choosing integrity when shortcuts tempt you.

The goal was never to look spiritual. It was to finish with character intact, heart aligned, and purpose fulfilled. Finishing well in faith means staying close to Jesus through every season—victory, failure, growth, and rebuilding.

The Goal Was Never Religion—It Was Relationship

If there is one truth I hope stays with you long after you close this book, it is this: Jesus did not rescue you to place you under heavier pressure. He rescued you to walk with you.

Religion can train behavior. Relationship transforms identity. Religion measures performance. Relationship builds trust. Religion asks, "Did I do enough?" Relationship asks, "Did I stay close?"

That difference reshapes how you approach every day. When your focus shifts from performance to proximity, peace replaces pressure. You stop keeping score and start cultivating connection. You stop striving for approval and start living from acceptance.

The entire point of the Gospel is not behavior management—it is restored relationship. Jesus did not give His life to create more religious stress. He gave His life to restore communion. When that truth anchors you, obedience becomes response, not requirement. Discipline becomes desire, not duty.

Faith Is Built in the Same Place Championships Are Won

In elite sports, championships are not secured on game day. They are forged long before the crowd shows up. They're built in early-morning workouts when it would be easier to stay in bed. In quiet film sessions where adjustments are made. In recovery days that protect longevity. In disciplined habits repeated consistently.

Faith grows the same way.

Spiritual maturity is not produced by occasional inspiration. It grows through daily surrender. Through private prayer when no one hears your words. Through honest repentance that reshapes your heart. Through steady obedience in small things. Through returning again and again when you drift.

There are no cameras in those moments. No applause. No scoreboard flashing validation. Just you and God. That is where real transformation happens. The unseen work shapes visible impact. The private disciplines strengthen public integrity. The quiet decisions build enduring character.

You Will Have Off-Seasons—and That's Not Failure

Every serious athlete understands the rhythm of seasons. There are seasons of preparation and seasons of competition. Seasons of momentum and seasons of recovery. Growth never happens at one speed.

Faith follows the same pattern.

You will experience seasons of strength and seasons of dryness. Moments of clarity and moments of confusion. Times when you feel deeply connected and times when you feel distant. These fluctuations do not mean you've failed. They mean you're human.

What matters most is not flawless consistency. It is the habit of returning. Returning when you drift. Returning when you doubt.

Returning when you grow tired. Jesus is not asking for perfect performance. He is inviting faithful return.

Finishing the race the right way means understanding that endurance is built through rhythm. It means accepting that off-seasons are part of formation. It means trusting that even in quiet or confusing stretches, God is still shaping something deeper.

You may stumble. You may slow down. But as long as you keep returning, you are still in the race—and that is what finishing well is all about.

Don't Confuse Momentum With Maturity

Early in my life, I chased momentum. I chased the adrenaline of big moments, the rush of visible progress, the feeling of being in motion. In my career, achievement became the primary metric. In my early faith journey, I even confused emotional highs with spiritual depth. If it felt powerful, I assumed it was growth. If it moved quickly, I assumed it was progress.

But over time, experience corrected me.

Momentum is exciting—but it's temporary. Maturity is steady—and it endures. Emotion rises and falls. Relationship sustains through both victory and valley. There were seasons when everything in my world looked active and impressive, yet beneath that motion there was little stability. And there were quieter seasons that felt slower on the surface but were forming something stronger inside.

True peace does not mean circumstances are easy. It means you are aligned. It means your heart is anchored in something deeper than performance or perception. When your life is aligned with your Creator, intensity becomes less important than integrity. The flash of momentum loses its grip. The steady growth of maturity becomes the goal.

Alignment lasts. Hype fades. And if you want to finish well, maturity will carry you much farther than momentum ever could.

Church Matters—When It Strengthens Relationship

I believe deeply in the local church. I am actively part of a healthy, vibrant church community, and I am grateful for it. Community matters. Accountability matters. Shared worship, shared growth, shared mission—these are gifts.

But clarity matters too.

The right church strengthens your relationship with Jesus. The wrong system subtly replaces it. That distinction is crucial. A healthy church consistently points you toward Christ, not toward its own brand or personality. It equips believers to walk confidently with God rather than keeping them dependent on leadership. It creates space for authentic growth instead of fear-based compliance. It honors conscience and maturity rather than enforcing rigid conformity.

Community is powerful. It sharpens you, encourages you, stretches you. But your anchor must always remain Jesus Himself. Stay rooted in life-giving fellowship. Just make sure your foundation is not the system—it is the Savior.

When church deepens relationship, it becomes a training ground. When it replaces relationship, it becomes a substitute. And substitutes never sustain what only intimacy can.

Your Calling Is Bigger Than You—but It Flows Through You

God did not rescue you to sit on the sidelines. But He also did not rescue you to exhaust yourself trying to prove something. Calling will involve people. It will involve responsibility. It will involve influence that grows and stewardship that stretches you.

Calling is bigger than you. But it flows through you. And that means your alignment matters more than your activity.

You will encounter opportunities that stretch your capacity. You will feel the weight of responsibility. You will sense influence expanding in ways that challenge your comfort. But none of it is meant to be carried alone, and none of it is meant to pull you away from intimacy.

If your assignment consistently distances you from Jesus, something is misaligned. If ambition repeatedly robs you of peace, the pace is unsustainable. If visible success requires sacrificing closeness with Christ, the cost is too high.

Calling thrives when it flows from relationship. It collapses when it tries to replace it. When your identity is secure in Him, your influence becomes healthier. When your heart is anchored, your leadership becomes steadier. And when your calling flows from closeness, it carries life—not just momentum.

That is the balance. That is the maturity. And that is how you build something that lasts.

Finish Close

When my coaching career eventually concludes, when the speaking engagements gradually diminish, when these books fade from memory, and when the platforms fall silent, there will still be one question that outweighs every accomplishment and every accolade: Did I walk faithfully with Jesus?

Not perfectly. Not impressively. Not in a way that earned applause.

But faithfully—with steady, unwavering commitment.

As competitors, we're trained to measure wins, trophies, championships, and milestones. We're conditioned to chase measurable outcomes and visible success. But the longer I walk with Christ, the clearer it becomes that heaven measures differently. The true scoreboard isn't public—it's personal. It's built in quiet obedience, private surrender, and daily alignment.

In the end, titles won't matter. Influence won't matter. Even legacy, as the world defines it, won't matter. What will matter is closeness. Did I stay near? Did I keep returning? Did I guard relationship over reputation? That is the only finish line worth pursuing. And it's a finish line available to every single one of us, every single day.

Final Reflection

Are you chasing temporary momentum—or are you building lasting endurance with Jesus?

Momentum feels exciting. It's visible. It moves fast. It impresses people. But endurance is quieter. It's formed in hidden places. It's sustained when motivation fades and emotions fluctuate. Endurance doesn't need hype—it needs relationship.

Take an honest look at your current pace. Are you driven by what looks successful, or anchored in what will sustain you? One produces highlights. The other produces depth.

Final Heart Check

What specific changes would allow your faith to feel lighter and deeper at the same time?

Lighter doesn't mean less serious. It means less performance pressure. Deeper doesn't mean more complicated. It means more aligned. Sometimes faith feels heavy because we've layered expectations, comparisons, and religious noise on top of a relationship that was meant to bring life.

Where could you simplify?

Where could you slow down?

Where could you trade striving for surrender?

Often, the shift isn't dramatic. It's intentional. It's choosing presence over pressure and trust over control.

Final Action Step

Today, don't focus on doing something that merely looks spiritual. Do something profoundly relational.

Sit in quiet presence for a few minutes. Put down the checklist. Resist the urge to perform. Listen with your whole heart. Breathe deeply and intentionally. Invite Jesus fully into the moment you're already experiencing.

You don't need the perfect words. You don't need a polished prayer. Just be honest. Just be present.

No performance pressure.

No religious obligation.

Just transformative presence.

That's where strength is rebuilt. That's where peace settles in. That's where faith becomes real again.

A Coach's Final Challenge

You don't need to prove your worth to anyone. You don't need to frantically catch up to some imagined timeline. You don't need to perform for approval. The greatest freedom I've discovered is this: the One who matters most has already chosen you.

So stay close.

One deliberate step.

One intentional day.

One brutally honest prayer at a time.

And when you inevitably drift—and you will—return without hesitation. That's not weakness. That's not failure. That's relationship. Champions don't quit when they stumble; they realign and keep moving. The same is true in faith.

Finish the race with determination. Finish aligned with your purpose. Finish close to your Creator.

Because faith ultimately wins not through hype, intensity, or image—but through endurance, humility, and intimacy. And finishing close to Jesus isn't just success for a season. It's victory for eternity.

CONCLUSION

STILL WALKING

If you've made it this far, it's because something inside you was already moving. Not toward more religion. Not toward another system to manage. But toward something authentic, life-giving, and deeply transformative. You didn't turn these pages because you needed more information. You kept reading because you were hungry for connection.

These words were never meant to hand you another script to memorize or a new routine to master. They were written as an invitation—an invitation into a deeper way of living that is anchored in relationship, not performance.

Maybe you were exhausted from constantly trying to measure up. Maybe you stayed faithful on the outside but felt empty on the inside. Maybe you've always loved Jesus, yet sensed a quiet distance you couldn't explain. Or maybe you believed, but knew there had to be more than routines, rules, and religious motion.

Whatever brought you here, one truth stands firm: you weren't searching for more religious effort. You were searching for genuine relationship. And that longing is not weakness. It's evidence that your heart was designed for more than performance. It was designed for presence.

This Was Never About Doing More

This journey was never about trying harder. It was never about becoming more impressive, more disciplined, or more spiritual looking. And it was certainly never about fixing yourself through sheer willpower. It has always been about returning—again and again—to the relationship.

Jesus doesn't want your performance. He desires your presence. He is not impressed by perfectly structured prayers or meticulously executed spiritual habits. He is moved by honesty. He responds to humility. He draws near to the person who chooses closeness over control.

Religion teaches behavior management. Relationship teaches belonging. Religion says, "Do better." Relationship says, "Come closer." And belonging changes everything about how you live, lead, love, and recover when you fail. When you belong, obedience shifts from obligation to alignment. You don't try to earn proximity. You rest in it.

You Don't Graduate From Relationship

One of the most damaging ideas in spiritual life is the belief that maturity means you eventually need Jesus less. That as you grow, you become more self-sufficient, more independent, more capable on your own.

The truth is the opposite.

Spiritual maturity means you depend on Him more freely, not less. You listen more intentionally. You return more quickly when you drift. You rest more deeply instead of striving harder. The strongest believers aren't the most independent—they are the most surrendered.

Relationship is not a starting block you outgrow. It is the center you continually return to. There is no advanced level where you no longer need presence, prayer, humility, or dependence. The deeper you go, the more you realize that closeness is not elementary—it is everything.

If You're Still Struggling, You're Not Failing

If parts of your story still feel unresolved… if faith still feels awkward some days… if doubt shows up unexpectedly… if healing seems slower than you hoped… you have not failed.

You are living real faith.

Relationship does not eliminate struggle; it reframes it. It means you are no longer carrying it alone. Jesus is not intimidated by unfinished stories. He doesn't withdraw because your progress feels messy. He is present inside the process.

Your questions don't scare Him. Your weakness doesn't repel Him. Your wounds don't disqualify you. In fact, those very places often become the doorway to deeper intimacy. The struggle doesn't push Him away—it invites Him in.

If Religion Hurt You, Jesus Still Welcomes You

If religious systems wounded you… if leaders misrepresented Jesus… if church became a place of pressure instead of healing… hear this clearly: Jesus is not who hurt you.

He sees what happened. He grieves what happened. And He heals gently.

You don't need to rush your recovery. You don't need to rebuild trust overnight. You don't need to pretend the damage didn't matter. Healing takes time. Discernment grows slowly. But your relationship with Jesus remains untouched by human failure.

Even if people distorted Him, He remains who He has always been—faithful, steady, and near.

Relationship Changes Everything

When you choose relationship, everything begins to shift from the inside out. Obedience becomes alignment instead of obligation. Prayer becomes conversation instead of ceremony. Community becomes authentic connection instead of performance. Faith becomes something you live, not something you manage.

Not because you suddenly become stronger. Not because you try harder. But because you stay closer.

Closeness does the transforming. Over time, it reshapes your motives, steadies your emotions, and refines your leadership. It turns frantic striving into confident trust. It replaces pressure with peace. And it grounds you when circumstances try to shake you.

This Is Not the End

This moment is not a finish line. It's a daily invitation.

You will have days when you drift. Days when you forget. Days when old patterns resurface and emotions run louder than faith. And Jesus will still be there.

Every return matters. Every honest prayer matters. Every small step toward Him carries eternal weight. You don't have to restart your faith from scratch every time you stumble. You simply return.

That's not weakness. That's relationship.

A Final Word

Christianity was never meant to be impressive. It was meant to be intimate. Not about appearing spiritual—but about walking honestly. Not about mastering rules—but about knowing a Person. Not about perfection—but about presence.

Wherever you find yourself right now—strong or weary, confident or uncertain—Jesus is not asking you to catch up. He is inviting you to walk with Him.

One step.

One day.

One honest moment at a time.

And that is enough.

Not because you are perfect—but because He is present. And the relationship remains gloriously, powerfully open.

www.ingramcontent.com/pod-product-compliance
Lightning Source LLC
Chambersburg PA
CBHW071739150726
47998CB00005B/1718